Never Mad Again

The Transformational Guide to Live in Peace

By:

James Fontaine

BALBOA.
PRESS

A DIVISION OF HAY HOUSE

ISBN: 978-1-4525-4773-2 (sc)
ISBN: 978-1-4525-4772-5 (e)
ISBN: 978-1-4525-4774-9 (hc)

Library of Congress Control Number: 2012903314

Balboa Press books may be ordered through booksellers or by contacting:

Balboa Press
A Division of Hay House
1663 Liberty Drive
Bloomington, IN 47403
www.balboapress.com
1-(877) 407-4847

Because of the dynamic nature of the Internet, any web addresses or links contained in this book may have changed since publication and may no longer be valid. The views expressed in this work are solely those of the author and do not necessarily reflect the views of the publisher, and the publisher hereby disclaims any responsibility for them.

The author of this book does not dispense medical advice or prescribe the use of any technique as a form of treatment for physical, emotional, or medical problems without the advice of a physician, either directly or indirectly. The intent of the author is only to offer information of a general nature to help you in your quest for emotional and spiritual well-being. In the event you use any of the information in this book for yourself, which is your constitutional right, the author and the publisher assume no responsibility for your actions.

Any people depicted in stock imagery provided by Thinkstock are models, and such images are being used for illustrative purposes only.
Certain stock imagery © Thinkstock.

Printed in the United States of America

Balboa Press rev. date: 2/27/2012

James Fontaine

www.nevermadagain.com

Twitter @nevermadagain.com

To my Wife who has always been my support, this book wouldn't have been possible without her.

To my kids, my best teachers.

CONTENTS

PREFACE   xi

INTRODUCTION   xv

Chapter I: WHEN ANGER TAKES CONTROL   1

Chapter II: ACCEPTING THAT WE WANT TO QUIT
                 GETTING ANGRY   7

Chapter III: LANGUAGE: THE MAIN PART OF ANGER   11

Chapter IV: BELIEVE IT IS POSSIBLE TO QUIT
                 GETTING ANGRY   15

Chapter V: DO WE NEED TO FORGIVE?   21

Chapter VI: ANGER IS A PRODUCT OF FEAR   25

Chapter VII: WHO IS CONTROLLING ANGER INSIDE
                 OF ME?   31

Chapter VIII: DISCUSSIONS   43

Chapter IX: WHY DO WE GET MAD WITH OURSELVES? 53

Chapter X: BLAME   61

Chapter XI: LISTEN   71

Chapter XII: EDUCATE CHILDREN WITHOUT
                 GETTING MAD   77

Chapter XIII: WORKING WITH THE EGO   83

Chapter XIV: MEDITATION TECHNIQUES   91

Chapter XV: FINDING THE SPIRITUAL SIDE OF ANGER 109

Chapter XVI: THE MOST IMPORTANT TIME IS "NOW"   115

PREFACE

Is getting angry good or bad?

If it is neither good nor bad, then why write a book about learning how to stop getting angry?

Generally speaking, we cannot classify emotions as good or bad—they are only what they are: emotions.

Emotions are our reaction to an external stimulus that is linked to an internal one, but it cannot simply be a matter of good or bad emotions because our body has its own wisdom from thousands of years and knows how to react to those stimuli.

Nothing of what our body does is bad—everything it does is from its source of wisdom, the same wisdom that knows perfectly how to pump an exact amount of blood with each heartbeat. It is the same wisdom that distinguishes proteins from carbohydrates and fats and distributes each to the organs that need them.

There aren't good or bad emotions; there are only emotions that feel well or emotions that don't feel good.

When something makes us feel happy, we have an emotion that feels good, but when someone bothers us or makes us angry, we have an emotion that feels bad.

Many experts recommend not repressing the emotions; they say that if you repress emotions, they can be transformed into diseases or can make you "explode" when you can no longer repress them. In Jim Carey's movie *Me, Myself and Irene,* Carey plays a character that has repressed his anger for many years until the day comes when he explodes and expresses all the anger he had repressed against others. Of course it is just a film full of fantasy, but it helps us understand what experts want to tell us about suppressing emotions.

The repressed emotions can accumulate in our body until the body expresses itself differently.

But if emotions are neither good nor bad, but only make us feel good or bad, and we know that repressing emotions is harmful to our health, what can we do to avoid the emotions that make us feel bad, without repressing them?

To answer this question we have to remember that emotions are produced by an external stimulus that is linked to an internal one. Very often we cannot control external stimuli because they are part of situations that happen in everyday life; what we can control is the internal stimulus that causes our body to activate the emotion.

The internal stimulus is different in each person and is based on the accumulation of past experiences, which are brought to the present, therefore generating specific emotions. If a person walking down the street sees a car running a red light, the person might be bothered by what he or she saw.

The external stimulus is the car that runs the red light, the internal stimulus is an association of ideas that makes the observer angry; maybe this person recalled an accident when a car ran a red light, or perhaps he or she remembers a TV show in which a car that ran a red light caused an accident.

At the same moment, let's say, another person across the street sees the car run the red light, but it doesn't bother him, perhaps because he has also done the same in an emergency situation; or maybe he saw that there were no other cars in the area. This person goes on his way without being bothered.

Both people experienced the same situation at the same time, but one of them was bothered and the other was not. The external stimulus could not have been controlled by either of them—but the inner stimulus could. Both decided *unconsciously* how to react, based on their personal story.

If this had happened in India, nobody would have been bothered that someone ran a red light—many people do it, and other people do not react with anger because they've learned that running a red light is common in their country.

This really is the key: to reach the point where external situations do not bother us the way they do now; to learn how to consciously react in each situation, therefore ensuring that in the future we could react unconsciously (or automatically) in similar situations. In that moment our unconscious mind will analyze the situation in a different way, so that what used to bother us before we will now see without anger.

This is different than repressing emotions. It is learning to understand why we got upset before and to gain new knowledge so that what used to bother us before no longer bothers us and to know that it is within our power to live free of argument, to know were not born with genes that make us grumpy, and to know that our parents are not guilty for our constantly being angry, and neither is society.

What I want to show you is a simple path to a life without anger so that you may have emotions that feel good and that the ones that feel bad disappear; at the same time I will show you a way toward wisdom so that you can stop blaming others and stop feeling guilty for what you do or for what you did not do in the past.

I want you to acquire the wisdom needed to live in peace and in a happy way most of the time, and I want you to do it unconsciously, without thinking about it.

The ultimate goal of this book is that when you look back at yourself you will see the way you used to be and no longer recognize that person; but you will see that "old" you with deep love and appreciation for having been that way—which has led you to be who you are now. I want you to realize in that moment the wisdom you have acquired, which is now part of your being.

I want you to be able to live, from that moment, free from anger.

INTRODUCTION

I am never upset for the reason I think.

- A Course in Miracles

THE ONLY REASON IN THE WORLD YOU GET MAD IS BECAUSE YOU THINK YOU ARE RIGHT, AND THE OTHER PERSON IS WRONG.

So simple, so easy—this is the only reason you get mad. If you really understand this, your whole life will change.

In fact, if you decide to stop reading this book, having understood this message, I invite you to do so, for if you fully understood it, you do not need to read the book, just go and apply its lesson to your life.

Now, if you are one of those who will continue reading the book, it is very likely that you're a little skeptical that the message can be so simple.

You may look at the sentence in different ways:

- It may be true

- It is too easy

- I can tell you several hundred reasons why I'm angry

- He does not live my life—I have a thousand reasons to be angry

- I do not believe it

- It is impossible

- Just one reason?

Believe me, I was the one who thought all these things when I heard the phrase for the first time on a radio show; unfortunately I don't know who said it, to give due credit.

I was driving along, scanning stations, when suddenly I heard the phrase:

THE ONLY REASON IN THE WORLD YOU GET MAD IS BECAUSE YOU THINK YOU ARE RIGHT, AND THE OTHER PERSON IS WRONG.

I must say, it captured my attention, but it seemed too simple to be true. I kept hearing the radio, but I could not really hear more; in my head I only heard reasons that I could get angry. I was trying to prove that what this person had just said was false—it could not be true. So my mind started to bomb me with all the reasons why I could be angry just because someone thought different from me.

But none of those reasons could contradict what I had heard: all the reasons I thought of took me to the same place. SOMEONE DID NOT THINK AS I DID AT THAT MOMENT, AND THAT MADE ME MAD.

If it were that simple, I thought to myself, anyone could know the reason why, at that moment, he feels angry or full of rage.

A few blocks later, after a deep search for reasons, I realized that the radio show was over. By that time it was a magical phrase for me; I could not contradict it in any way.

It was true!

It is simple, and if you understand it could become easy too, but in order to fully comprehend it we need to understand the nature of anger, and how it manifests in ourselves.

What is Anger?

Definition of Anger in English: it is an emotion. The physical effects of anger include increased heart rate, blood pressure, and levels of adrenaline and noradrenalin some view anger as part of the brain response to the perceived threat of harm.

None of the sensations that we experience when we are angry is pleasant. I am not saying anger is all-wrong; all emotions have a specific function, which is tell us something through our body. Anger is a body reaction to an external situation, but it is not a feeling we like; however, it can become addictive to the body, which needs these chemicals to feel well when it does not know something better.

From childhood we are taught that anger is bad, that people who get angry are not good, and that we must control our anger. We are taught that to suppress our anger so that other people do not see that we are angry and do not consider us bad people.

Currently there are many studies that tell us that repressing emotions can make us sick, that our body is trying to tell us something, to teach us something with every emotion that comes up, and that if we do not listen to it, the body will find a more intense form in which to express it. That is why, if we repress emotions, our body may begin to speak to us through illness. In the beginning it could be a simple cold, but if we keep ignoring it, it could become cancer.

But if anger is not bad (although not pleasant) and its repression makes us sick, then what have we learned? What can we do to not get angry?

It seems confusing, but the answer is very simple:

YOU GET MAD BECAUSE YOU THINK YOU ARE RIGHT, AND THE OTHER PERSON IS WRONG.

If we know in advance why we get angry, then we can see each situation from another point of view. We can then reduce the number of times we get angry, without repressing our anger, but by looking with different eyes at the situations that made us angry. We will then feel fewer unpleasant emotions and live more happily than we do now, coexist easily with those around us, and see life with greater wisdom.

CHAPTER I

WHEN ANGER TAKES CONTROL

THE ONLY REASON IN THE WORLD YOU GET MAD IS BECAUSE YOU THINK YOU ARE RIGHT, AND THE OTHER PERSON IS WRONG.

The easiest way to understand this is with examples, but do not limit yourself with the ones I purpose: make your own list and fill it with all the reasons why you get angry. As other reasons come to mind, add them to the list.

As you fill the list, you may run out of options, which are repeated each time but take you to the same place: *Someone was not thinking the way you want them to think—that is, your way.*

Let's start with something simple and common:

SITUATION I

You are in your car and you come to a cross-street where you have the right of way, but another car also approaching the intersection does not stop, in fact he accelerates in order to cross the intersection first.

Fortunately you are able to stop. You put your head out the window and yell at the other driver.

Let's analyze the situation in detail:

You are really angered about the incident. If you could, you would have punched the guy who did this to you and you think, "How come he did not see what he did to me, he could have hit me, I have my children with me, and something serious could have happened to them!"

Here it appears that you are angry that the other guy did something wrong—he even broke the law. Therefore, you are angry about his actions.

This seems to be the reason, but let's continue analyzing in order to see all the layers of the situation.

You are the one that thinks the other did something wrong, but probably the guy does not think he did something wrong.

You can also argue that he broke the law and that many others besides you believe what he did is wrong.

At this point I would like to add something. There are probably a lot more people who think like you, It is likely that someone standing on the corner may have seen what happened and was also angry, but the meaning does not change: the driver was angry because someone else thought differently from him.

If you believe that he did something wrong, then what should he have done?

In your opinion, he should have yielded the right of way, let you pass, and then moved on.

That of course was exactly what he did not do; in fact he did the opposite of what you thought he should do.

What bothered you deeply is that he did not do what you wanted him to do or, put a little differently: he did not do what you thought was good, therefore *he thought differently from you.* If he had yielded the right of way to you, you both would have been thinking the same way and you would not have been angry with him.

SITUATION II

It is Valentine's Day and a lovely woman prepares a romantic dinner to surprise her husband. She prepares a delicious meal, giving attention to every detail, and putting out the best wine, too. She dresses up for the occasion, lights the candles, and waits for her husband to arrive.

Usually he comes home by 5:30 on Thursdays so she has everything ready at 5:00. But at 5:45 he has not arrived, however, it is only 15 minutes, nothing to worry about. Then it is 6:30 and she starts to worry—maybe something could have happened to him. But does not want to call him and ruin the surprise.

At 7:30 she decides to call him, but he does not answer the phone, and by this time she is angry; the romantic dinner no longer means anything to her, she just wants to know why he has not arrived, where he has been, and why he did not have the courtesy to call and say where he was.

Finally at 9:00 he comes home, walks in and finds his wife in pajamas, watching TV, with the table still set for dinner.

She reproaches him for all she went through to make that dinner. Then she goes to bed, still very mad at him, and without having had a romantic dinner. She tells him he has no excuse. She is really mad at him.

Let's analyze the situation in detail:

She is angry with her husband because he arrives late on Valentine's Day, when she had prepared a romantic dinner for two. She really wanted to surprise him and in return got no consideration from him. He did something wrong when he did not show up on time.

This is one of the simplest cases. Let's get to the bottom of it and discover the real reason why she got mad.

Her husband did not know that dinner was going to be a surprise, so he was not thinking what his wife was thinking.

What she thought is that he should have arrived early so that the two of them could have a romantic dinner, or at least that he could have called to say he would be late, in which case she would delayed starting the dinner.

"What was he thinking—today is Valentine's Day, the day for being with your partner and showing the love you have for each other."

That is the way she believes he should have thought; but he was not thinking as she was, and at the end of the day that is what made her angry.

She was not angry when she made the dinner—she was happy at that time, she thought he was going to arrive early for dinner, and she believed he thought just the way she did, and that did not make her angry, it made her happy. But the moment it became clear that he did *not* think like her, she got mad.

SITUATION III

Your son has not cleaned up his room for days. You come in and see everything thrown around, you can barely walk, and there are dirty clothes on the floor, toys, and even food scraps.

You leave the room, furious, and yell at your son to come immediately, and he knows at once that you are angry:

"Why do you have that mess in your room?"

He only answers by raising his shoulders in a shrug.

His not having an answer bothers you even more, and you say:

"You are grounded for the whole weekend."

You leave him and go to the kitchen.

When your husband arrives, you stop him almost before he enters the house and tell him:

"Do you know what your son did this time?"

Obviously he does not know but he asks you to tell him what happened, but for you it is a rhetorical question.

You tell him that the boy did not pick up his room. You tell him how the room looked, and as the story goes on you are getting angrier and angrier as you remember the way you felt at that moment.

You tell him that you asked the boy why his room was such a mess and that he had not even answered, and then, because that made you even angrier, you had to ground him for the weekend.

Your husband did not see the room, but he says:

"He is just a child. It is hard for him to pick up his room by himself. I believe you overreacted when you grounded him."

That makes you even angrier! Now you are not only angry with your son, you are also angry with your husband because he did not understand you and did not support you in your decision.

Let's analyze the situation in detail:

In principle, you're upset with your child that he has not picked up his room the way you think it should be; but perhaps for him a messed-up room does not have any importance. In fact it is probable that he doesn't even see it as a mess.

What bothers you is not that the clothes and the toys are on the floor; what really bothers you is that you have an idea of how clean a room should be and your son's room did not reach your standard. In other words, your son does not have the same idea you have of a clean room.

It bothers you that your child did not pick up his room "well." But "well" is your idea of what is right or wrong, and this is what your son did not share with you.

THE ONLY REASON IN THE WORLD YOU GET MAD IS BECAUSE YOU THINK YOU ARE RIGHT, AND THE OTHER PERSON IS WRONG.

Then your husband came and you got mad at him because he did not share your idea about how to educate your son.

"How come he told me I was wrong if he was not there when it happened? He did not see the room as I did."

You do not really care if your husband is right or wrong; what bothers you is that he did not think like you think, and you're convinced that in this situation the punishment you gave your son was right even though your husband thought it was excessive. You're convinced of what is right and wrong, and when he thinks differently, you get mad. If he had said that the punishment was right, then you would not have had any reason to be angry.

This is one of the most obvious examples. When a couple disagrees on the education of children, they usually get mad because one of them thinks differently than the other.

When others think like we do, we feel empathy rather than anger, but if that same person thinks differently about something else, then we get angry.

CHAPTER II

ACCEPTING THAT WE WANT TO QUIT GETTING ANGRY

IF YOU ACCEPT THAT SOMETHING IS WRONG, THEN YOU CAN CHANGE IT.

A lot of people can't change because they just don't accept the situation they don't like. There are many people who are trying to convince themselves that a few cigarettes a day will not cause any damage; others try to convince themselves that they are not overweight, even though they are; others make believe that they do not need to exercise because they already feel good, or they are convinced they have no time to exercise.

When you really accept it, then you can change, otherwise, you are just "trying" to change, but you don't get results.

As I mentioned above, it is not necessary to accept that getting angry is wrong, just accept that is an unpleasant feeling, one that you want to change.

The next step is to accept that the reason you get angry is that someone thinks differently than you think. I don't ask you to completely accept this at this time, it will come to you, as we go through the chapters, you will comprehend it.

Now if at this point you've already accepted and you are convinced that it is true, then continue reading the book to discover more and more, so that you can eradicate your anger for good.

Remember that the most important part is the acceptance; you want to feel less angry every time, right? Now that you already have the book in your hands (or in your e-reader) it means you really want to.

But this is really not that simple. Many of us are used to getting and being angry, our body has become addicted to substances that are secreted each time we get angry.

Inside our brains are neural cells that help us learn, remember, as well as to handle all our other bodily tasks.

When nerve cells fire together they wire together; if you practice something over and over for a certain period of time, those cells create a long-term relationship, they create canal-like structures on your brain and they make nets that get reinforced every time you repeat the action.

That is the way we learned how to walk or talk, and also the way someone masters an action, such as a sport.

When you get angry over and over again, neural cells connect to each other and create long-term relationships. Once a long-term relationship is created, you act automatically in the same situation—it's as if you have no control over that situation. That's why we *react* in a certain situation.

The word itself has its own definition: We repeat the action from other times we acted—we have literally taught our brains how to act in a certain situation.

Besides those neural cells, which create long-term relationships, there are chemical substances created by our body each time we have an emotion.

A part of the brain called the hypothalamus is the most sophisticated chemical factory known to man. It produces different chemicals for each emotion we have. These chemicals are called peptides.

Peptides are small chains of amino acid sequences that travel to the body's cells through the bloodstream.

All the cells in our body have hundreds of receptors searching for these peptides. When peptides get to the cell the cell locks it in. When cells lock in the peptides, the cells are changed in different ways.

When cells get used to specific peptides, they get "addicted" to them. Because they can only get them if the same emotion is experienced again, the body tries to recreate the emotion in order to get the same chemical response.

Dr. Candace Pert named the peptides and through her research explained the way they work in our bodies.

Therefore it is likely that many of us are addicted to anger. It may seem unbelievable, but it is true. Many of us have addictions to negative things such as alcohol, cigarettes, rejection, anger, and so on.

How can anyone have an addiction to anger? All of us want to feel good all the time, don't we? Well, everybody knows that smoking is not good for our health and yet there are millions of people who smoke. It's not that we consciously became addicted to something; we got addicted because we did something repeatedly, thus forming a habit. It takes only twenty-one days for our neurons to form connections that did not previously exist—in other words, to form a habit.

This is how we become addicted to something; we do not <u>really</u> notice, it is so subtle we do not perceive it

In many ways, we reinforce our addictions with our language and the way we express ourselves to others. Without noticing it, we are reinforcing our addictions, as we will see in the next chapter.

For now just think about anger as something you want to quit feeling in your life.

CHAPTER III

LANGUAGE: THE MAIN PART OF ANGER

The way we speak to ourselves or to others has an influence on how we behave. Not knowing the right way to use language can be the cause of anger.

In neuro-linguistic programming (NLP) there are three very simple principles that help us to communicate our ideas properly:

1. The brain does not understand the word "not"

2. The brain has no sense of humor

3. The brain understands everything as it is said

Let's do a very simple exercise that will illustrate the first principle. I'm going to give you a very simple statement and I want you to follow the instructions:

"Do not imagine a pink elephant."

What happened?

I clearly said, "Do not imagine."

You couldn't follow the directive because your brain works with images in order to understand language, so in order to understand something you have to imagine it. In other words, the only way for you *not* to imagine a pink elephant is to imagine a pink elephant.

So if we analyze the statement, you did exactly the opposite. You imagined a pink elephant, which helps us to understand that your brain does not register the word "not." In this case it only understood the rest of the sentence, because the brain cannot create a clear image of "not."

So when we say ourselves:

"I'm not going to get angry today"

Our brain understands the order without recognizing the word "not," and thus:

"I'm going to get angry today"

The second and third principles are even more important than the first, and at the same time they go hand in hand.

If we tell our friends in a conversation:

"I am grumpy,"

Our brain does not understand that we probably said it only as a joke or in order to make an offhand comment. For the brain, what we have said is a claim that goes deep. If we constantly repeat it, our nerve cells start making a long-term relationship, which makes us believe it.

Our brain understands everything *as it is said,* it does not understand assumptions, it only understands by images. So if I tell my brain that "I'm grumpy," my brain displays the image of me getting angry; my brain does not have an interpretation and does not know if it is a joke or not, doesn't even know if what I say is the reality.

And that brings me to my next point: THE BRAIN DOES NOT KNOW THE DIFFERENCE BETWEEN WHAT IS HAPPENING OUTSIDE AND WHAT IS HAPPENING INSIDE; FOR THE BRAIN, EVERYTHING IS REALITY.

To understand that our brain does not distinguish reality in the outside any more than in the inside, let's make another experiment:

* Imagine you have in your hand a big juicy lime, imagine that you feel its texture, you see its color, with a knife you cut it in half and you see and feel how juicy it is; you feel drops of juice falling through your fingers. Now you take it to your mouth, squeeze it and taste it, and it is sour, very sour.

You notice that the lime never existed; it only existed in your imagination. But even though it is an imaginary lime, you also notice you have saliva in your mouth—just from imagining the juicy, sour lime.

It is the same with our thoughts; it is not necessary that something be true in order for the brain to believe in it. Our words are more powerful than we can imagine, they can change the way our brain reacts to external events—we can really believe in something that is not true making us react in a way we do not recognize.

So if our parents didn't know this when we were little, they could have said to us or to other people:

"My son always gets angry, he has an explosive personality"

"He has his father's bad temper"

Our brains made the neural-cell connections to record that pattern, and those words had more impact on us because they came from our parents, the people we love the most when we are little. It is even possible we believed that if they said something like that about us in front of their friends, then that is what they expected from us—to be angry all the time or to have our father's bad temper.

Then we would notice that our parents got mad at us because of our anger, and we would see that that was a contradiction. In the end, we found that we had their attention when we got mad—good attention or bad attention, it didn't matter which; it is enough for a child to have attention, period. So we would get angry in order to get our parents' attention.

Then we got the idea that we had a bad temper and kept saying to our friends:

"If I get angry, watch out!"

"I can't control my anger; I think it is because I inherited from my father"

Then when we went to work and any little thing we did not like made us angry, after a while others had the idea that we had a bad temper. Even our boss would think of us as mad people when he referred to us, therefore reinforcing the idea we had a bad temper.

So for years we have strengthened the idea that are, without a doubt, the way we are:

"I get angry often; this is how I am. If someone loves me, they will have to accept me the way I am"

I want you to know deep inside of you that you are not angry all the time, you did not inherit your father's bad temper, you just did not know this:

THE ONLY REASON IN THE WORLD YOU GET MAD IS BECAUSE YOU THINK YOU ARE RIGHT, AND THE OTHER PERSON IS WRONG.

CHAPTER IV

BELIEVE IT IS POSSIBLE TO QUIT GETTING ANGRY

If you believe it's possible, you are right, and if you believe that it is impossible, you're right.

Henry Ford

THE ONLY REASON IN THE WORLD YOU GET MAD IS BECAUSE YOU THINK YOU ARE RIGHT, AND THE OTHER PERSON IS WRONG.

If we reinforce the idea by practicing it for a certain period of time and work constantly to reinforce the idea the same way our other ideas were reinforced many years ago, the brain begins gradually making new neural-cell connections, and those that are not used lose their connection. Then we have a new subconscious pattern—but one that we put in place consciously.

Fortunately, our brain has one mechanism that I call the "self-defense mechanism" which works by disabling neurological connections that are not used. I've always believed that the brain does this because it would be very difficult to live with the losses we have over the course of our lives if we remembered everything all the time.

Remember when you left school, your friends were the most important thing in your life; you needed them even more than your parents, you were inseparable. You made a promise never to separate and that your friendship would last forever. At that time you would never have believed that most of them would never show up in your life again.

But it happened: You tried to keep in touch; you even tried to get together and talked on the phone week after week. But after a year you only had contact with a few of them, the others were forgotten.

Your brain was breaking the neurological nets, the ones that kept you thinking about them and attached to them. Soon you stopped thinking about them, you did not need them anymore, even the friend who was indispensable to you at a certain point in your life. It also happens with failed romances, places you lived—even with the loss of loved ones.

When connections disappear, it does not mean we forget; that kind of memory is different to the neural connections that made you need them in the first place. It doesn't mean we don't love them anymore; love comes from the heart, not the brain. It only means you do not need them in the same way you used to. Our brain activates its security system so we can continue with our lives: that's what I call the self-defense mechanism.

Many of us know people who have had a major loss in life and continue suffering for a long time, as if their self-protection system did not work. It works in all of us, but some people will not let it work correctly, they keep bringing the same thought back over and over and keeping the neurological connections intact. Sometimes these people believe that if they forget their loved ones, it will mean that they do not love them anymore.

Our brain understands everything literally; if we continue to nourish it with the same thoughts, it will continue reinforcing the neurological connections it has already established. If we gradually stop doing so, the brain will employ its self-defense system, and this will help us continue with our lives.

Some people think that if we tell our brain something we do not believe is true, it is like telling our brain a lie. But haven't we been telling lies for so long—lies we started believing gradually—that we no longer consider them lies but a part of which we think we are?

If you're not still convinced that THE ONLY REASON IN THE WORLD YOU GET MAD IS BECAUSE YOU THINK YOU ARE RIGHT, AND THE OTHER PERSON IS WRONG, it makes no difference: you can start telling this "lie" to your brain and see what happens.

You have nothing to lose, anyway; every time you get angry, you have unpleasant feelings, so you can start by "lying" to your brain at this moment, then see whether it works or not.

Just remember, the lemon never existed, but your brain took it as *real*, it even sent orders to different systems in your body to prepare to eat a lemon.

To begin to introduce this idea to your belief system, you can start telling your brain THE ONLY REASON IN THE WORLD YOU GET MAD IS BECAUSE SOMEONE THINKS DIFFERENTLY FROM THE WAY YOU THINK ten times in the morning and ten times a night for twenty-one days. According to some brain studies, it takes only twenty-one days to make new neural-cell connections. Although these connections will not be permanent at the end of the twenty-one days, we will already have taken the first step to believe in this idea, and if we keep *reinforcing* it, it will become permanent.

REINFORCE THE IDEA

The formation of new beliefs by the process of repeating affirmations (using our brain's ability to accept something as existing in our reality) is what I call the first step, because once there is a possibility in our brain for it to be true, we can go on with the process and embrace this new idea.

How do we reinforce it?

One way to reinforce beliefs is through feelings, which are a huge anchor. Our brain has to make neural cell nets, therefore reinforcing an idea.

Here is an experience that reaffirmed this idea in me:

Years ago, my parents took my sister and me to Disneyland in Anaheim, California. I was six years old, so for me, as for most children who visit this magical place for the first time, the visit was like a dream; it was like walking inside a movie and being the hero. This experience left a mark in my childhood, and in my life. Even now when we take our children to Disneyland, my wife says I am the one who is having more fun than the rest of the family.

Almost twenty years passed before I went back to Disneyland. I always wanted to return, but couldn't. It was only by coincidence, when a friend couldn't go on a trip with other friends, that I was invited to come along.

Once again, the trip was to Disneyland in Anaheim. At first, everything was good, but I didn't feel the magic I had felt as a child. Then we stepped into the Pirates of the Caribbean—and it happened: I smelled the air; I felt an unparalleled joy, a feeling of inexplicable peace, happiness and bliss, I felt the happiness, simplicity, and lightness of a six-year-old child. At that moment, I really knew I was in Disneyland!

How can a simple fragrance bring back so many feelings and memories? It was a fragrance I had perceived only a couple of times on my first trip, and that had been almost twenty years ago.

The answer is simple: the fragrance was stuck deep in my brain for a powerful anchor, the feelings.

Feelings are wonderful and powerful anchors that can help reinforce behaviors and attitudes. We also have other anchors, which we don't recognize, anchors that are there because of our past feelings, unconsciously implanted in our brains.

Have you ever seen a child crying loudly because someone has taken away his toy or his candy? He cries really loudly and there is nothing you can say at that moment that can make him crying. You can tell him it is not important, or that you are going to buy him more candy tomorrow, but he is not listening—he is only listening to his own thoughts.

It is the same with adults, or someone who is really angry. In that moment that person is only listening to his thoughts, nothing else. He is listening to his mind telling him why he should be angry or sorrowful, and he is trying to convince himself that something is really wrong and that he should be angry.

At that time he is not connected with the outside world, he is not listening to anything you say, he is in a hypnotic state, and anything you say will be in vain, even worst, he could take it personal and try to defend himself.

It's the same with us when we get angry, our mind is a hundred percent busy trying to find reasons why the other person did something wrong, trying to determine that we are right to be angry. We ignore what others are telling us, we do not see things clearly, and we perceive only a small part of reality.

At such times it will be hard to tell ourselves to calm down and realize that THE ONLY REASON IN THE WORLD I GET MAD IS BECAUSE I THINK I AM RIGHT, AND THE OTHER PERSON IS WRONG. In that moment everything is blocked because of our anger, and our attention is only focused in the anger.

This is not easy to do in those moments.

The way we strengthen the idea is to reinforce it *when we are calm* and we can actually sit down and think about what the other person did to make us angry and to remember that THE ONLY REASON IN THE WORLD YOU GET MAD IS BECAUSE YOU THINK YOU ARE RIGHT, AND THE OTHER PERSON IS WRONG.

If we are able to do this in peace every time we get angry, eventually we will be able to see it in those moments when we are getting mad.

As we move through the process, every time it will be a little easier to laugh at what made us angry and we can bring it closer to the moment of anger. There will be situations where, even when we are still angry, we realize that we are not angry at the other person's behavior, but that we are angry with that person because he did not think, as we wanted him to think.

This is a process that requires time so it can be imprinted in our subconscious mind. If we do it for twenty-one days, our brain will make neuronets, and if we keep doing it after this period, we will be reenforcing the idea, therefore the neuronets will become permanent and be a part of our subconscious mind, which is the first step for living in peace.

CHAPTER V

DO WE NEED TO FORGIVE?

I remember when I was little and I read the Bible in school. There was a passage where Jesus says:

"Forgive your brother seventy times seven"

"If your brother hits you on the cheek, offer him the other one"

The Bible told us that Jesus preached love and he said we ought to forgive those who hurt us, as often as necessary, and instead of defending ourselves, we should turn the other cheek. That didn't sound pleasant at all.

It seemed impossible for an eight-year-old child to follow the words of Jesus. In my child's mind, I could not accept that Jesus wanted me to suffer all the time—it would make me feel like a martyr if I had to turn the other cheek when someone hit me.

What he seemed to say was, if a classmate waited for the recess to bother me or beat me, I should not tell the teacher or defend myself, instead I should sit and wait to be hit and punched again, —and at the same time I should understand Jesus would be happy for what I was experiencing!

As I grew up I understood this concept better. Jesus never wanted to see us suffering, on the contrary Jesus was showing us a path to a higher consciousness beyond suffering; at the same time, he was showing us a way to find peace and happiness instead of suffering, a way that was within the reach of anyone, not just for Jesus or the saints.

I realized that rancor is the opposite of forgiveness and is what actually causes suffering; Jesus was showing us the way to eliminate rancor, suffering and find inner peace.

I believed Jesus wanted me to forgive the other at the moment when I was really angry and full of rancor. But the teaching of Jesus was much more than that. He teaches us that forgiveness sets us free from resentment and guilt and gives us peace—it makes us feel close to God. But forgiveness can't be an obligation because it is impossible to forgive someone just for the sake of an obligation. We can say the words, but at the same time not forgive, and therefore keep our feelings of rancor.

Jesus knew forgiveness is something that exists only with love. He knew we were imperfect human beings, but he also knew we were perfect beings beyond our body and beyond our mind—he knew that we are beings of light and knew that if we leave our egos behind, we can live in love's perfection.

Forgiveness, essentially, is a benefit for the one who forgives. It is one of life's greatest gifts. Even if we use forgiveness in a selfish way in order to feel good, we will still benefit from it.

Then how to practice forgiveness without feeling bad?

The easiest way is to stop feeling resentment. If we feel no resentment toward anyone, we will not have to forgive anyone.

Resentment by definition is *to feel it again*. Then if we have resentment we are repeating the same unpleasant feeling, and it happens only because we are remembering the past. Then resentment is to bring back the same unpleasant feeling from the past over and over.

How to stop feeling resentment?

The answer is as simple as the sentence we have been repeating, with a slight change:

The reason you feel resentment is because you think someone is wrong and you are right.

If you really know deep inside that someone else thinks differently from you, it doesn't make that person wrong. And because the chances are that they will never think as you do means that rancor need not exist.

This is much easier than trying to forgive someone when you feel resentment. In fact there are many couples and families, even nations that have been divided due to rancor.

I think the word forgiveness has over time been associated with a sense of guilt that comes from the belief that if we forgive someone, we are giving up and letting the other person humiliate us. If that is the case, then forgiveness is only for martyrs and saints. Of course, Jesus forgave those who spat on the cross because he was God and in God all things are possible. But if we try to think like Jesus and see others the way he did, then it is simple—he saw us with the eyes of love, and he always knew that we all think differently.

He even said it when he was on the cross:

"Father, forgive them for they do not know what they are doing"

I'm sure God forgives us always. He created us, so he knows what we are made of, he is aware we have an ego, which has a specific role in our life. He is also aware that we all think differently. Jesus said it so we could understand the idea that he was not angry with anyone, he loved us all. He knew well before he said those words that there would be many who would disagree with his words.

He knew that those who spat on him did so because they believed they were right. Jesus never had to forgive anyone because he never felt offended by anyone, never felt hatred for anyone. He loved everyone unconditionally and knew many would think differently than he did, therefore he was not angry with them.

This is how we can apply forgiveness in a different way, in a human way.

WE DON'T NEED TO FORGIVE ANYBODY IF WE ARE NOT ANGRY WITH ANYBODY.

If we recognize that someone else thinks differently from us—differently from what we believe is right or wrong—then our anger will disappear and we won't need to say, "I forgive you."

In this way, "I forgive you," means that we have forgiven the other person in our hearts. In these moments we start to feel good, even if the other person doesn't know we have forgiven her, we feel really good. This is why I say that forgiveness has a deeper impact on ourselves than on other people.

We believe forgiveness makes the other person feel good and we should forgive for the sake of the other person, but the one who suffers the most is the one who does not forgive.

The moment we understand forgiveness in this new way, we will start to feel the inner peace Jesus felt; we will feel the peace of God.

CHAPTER VI

ANGER IS A PRODUCT OF FEAR

I am an old man and have known a great many troubles, but most of them never happened.

Mark Twain

When you see someone who is angry, did you know that it is because he is afraid—even though he doesn't know it?

Why is anger a product of fear?

When the ego feels attacked, it feels the need to defend itself at any price because it is afraid of dying. The ego is afraid that you will realize that what you're thinking is not reality but rather an illusion made up by the ego. You are watching "reality" through the lens of your ego. Because the ego's main fear is of dying, it needs to convince you that you have a life-or-death need to defend yourself in order to survive—just as it does. The ego needs to know that it is right.

Fear is the opposite of love. Love is the perfect state of being.

A Course in Miracles tells us that love is real and that everything else, including fear, is unreal. Fear is the opposite of love; if there is love there can be no fear, and fear cannot exist in love because love is real and everything else is an illusion.

It was very hard for me to comprehend this. Why, in love, is there no fear? And will love be enough to make fear disappear?

Then one day I realized that the fear we feel is only the projection of the ego's fear of dying, its fear of annihilation. Our fear is not real; rather, we feel the ego's fear.

The ego lives in fear all the time. This is the fear, which *A Course in Miracles* tells us is the opposite of love, because the ego does not live on love, it lives on fear.

Love knows no fear, love is real, and the ego's fear is not real—in fact, the ego is not real, it is only an illusion of who we are. Therefore, if the ego is not real, then neither is its fear.

It's much easier to deal with fear if we are convinced that it is not real, if we know it is an illusion of the ego.

TWO DIFFERENT TYPES OF FEAR

There are two types of fear, ego-fear and physical fear.

We feel physical fear on rare occasions:

Physical fear is a real fear; for example, when we are about to fall from a high place, or just before a car crashes, we face this fear, which is a based on survival of the physical body and which triggers the body's systems, such as the secretion of adrenaline, to deal out the necessary tools to escape from danger.

This fear is shared with other animal species, which have similar mechanisms to defend them. Some of them have very different defense mechanisms. Snakes' mechanisms to get out of danger are different from those of deer. In both animals there are chemical reactions within the body that activate muscles, accelerate the heartbeat, and alert the senses.

Physical fear is real, but it is a fear that disappears after the danger is past. We remain slightly more alert while the body winds down from its reactions to the fear, but once the real danger is gone, the physical fear disappears.

Ego-fear is the fear we feel most of the times. It is a fear based on the past; stories about the chance to loose something we have, like status, possessions, titles and everything we believe we are or have.

Physical fear is a good thing: it prepares our body for an external situation. The fear of the ego is neither good nor bad, it simply does not exist; it is not real.

We believe the fear we feel is real, and many of us refuse to stop feeling fear because we believe it is a natural part of being a human being—and indeed, physical fear is natural.

There is a belief that says that if we give up fear, then if we have a dangerous situation we will not react appropriately to the danger because we would not feel fear. This is not true; it is only the ego defending itself, creating stories so it won't disappear. The ego creates "fear" to keep itself from feeling afraid of dying.

The reaction to danger is built into our system, engraved in our brain just like breathing or our heartbeat. It is very hard not to feel that fear. Even bullfighters that have many years of experience still feel afraid when they go in to fight the bulls. The same thing happens with cowboys and racecar drivers.

The good news is that we can control the reaction that causes this kind of fear. Bullfighters can control their reactions, but they still feel fear, for the rest of us, it would be almost impossible not to run away as fast as possible!

If we understand that being afraid to stop feeling fear is just another invented message of the ego, we will come closer to comprehending the true nature of this fear. This can help us change this fear into love. When we live in the present moment, fear does not exist, because in the present moment the ego does not exist. The present is real, fear is not.

LOVE DISSOLVES FEAR

Love recognizes that we all think differently and that we all have an ego inside of us, which is constantly trying to defend itself. Ego is in everybody, and every ego is different, but all of them are trying to survive. If we can accept this, we will begin to see others with new eyes, the eyes of love—for love can feel neither fear nor anger.

This should not be viewed as an obligation but as a belief, a knowing within us of how we really are and a desire to accept others as they are, and not the way the ego wants them to be.

The ego tries to change the way others think in order to think like it does, even on little things. But if we resist the ego's temptation, we could apply this idea:

"It is better to feel good than to be right"

The ego is the one who wants to be right and our being is the one who wants to feel good, or as Dr. Dyer says, "Wanting to feel good is synonymous with wanting to feel God."

As I mentioned earlier, Jesus always looked at us through the eyes of love and always saw us as beings that think differently, even though he accepted us just the way we are.

So if the ego is hurting us so much, should we be mad at the ego?

I believe not. If the ego did not exist, we would not be living human experiences, we would be pure spirit and our learning in this world would be null. This book is about letting go of the anger in the past. Getting mad at the ego would be like giving the ego a reason to live.

Ego is a part of the human being, part of nature, and part of the process of learning and enlightenment. It is also part of growing up and even has its rewards along the way, because every time we silence the ego, we feel closer to God and feel the peace of getting closer to our source of wisdom and happiness.

It is not a war *against* the ego; it is a job *with* the ego. If we see the ego as our enemy, a part of us that hates us and makes us feel bad, then we are listening to the ego! Remember that the ego only wants to live; it does not care if we feel bad. And if we feel bad because we hate the ego, then the ego feels good, knowing that as long as we recognize it by fighting against it, it will remain strong and alive.

We must look at the ego through the eyes of love, as Jesus sees us, knowing that we all think differently, knowing that we all have an ego inside of us which tells us how to see the world from its point of view. This is how we need to see the ego, as someone who thinks differently than we really do, or as a fearful child. Eventually, after we have no need of the ego, we will be grateful to it for being the best teacher we could have had, by helping us experience ourselves as perfect human beings.

CHAPTER VII

WHO IS CONTROLLING ANGER INSIDE OF ME?

Ego.

The ego is that which contains the consciousness, according to Freud.

If we accept Freud's definition, we realize that the ego does not have the consciousness within it, but it *contains* the consciousness, not letting it come out. It retains it so we don't know the truth, because if the consciousness knew the truth then the ego disappears; and the biggest fear of the ego, and its only reason to exist, is the fear of death. The ego does everything it can to avoid death. The ego is not like us, who are endless spirits; therefore ego has a reason to fear death. The ego is not endless, so if it dies, then that's it for the ego, and when the ego dies, the consciousness rises to the surface.

Ego is the idea we have of ourselves: our name, our skin and hair color, our religious beliefs, our social position, the title we've got, the job we have, our ideas of right and wrong, our possessions.

The ego wants to control others in order to avoid death. It feels that if it is right and others are not, then it is safe. Similarly, we get angry because someone else does not think like we want him to think—the key word is "want." This means that we wish to control the thoughts of others in order to make them think like we do.

But what happens if consciousness rises above the ego and realizes that everything the ego says is a lie? This can help us realize that the anger we feel is nothing more than the ego's desire to control the thoughts of others.

If we look at it this way, we realize that this is the greatest pride that exists, the desire to control how others think. And if we can't control the thoughts of others, we get angry. We are like that child who cries when he can't have his toy, kicks and throws himself on the ground in a tantrum.

The child's tantrum eventually affects others. Soon they begin to feel bad, too, so they give him back his toy to calm him down, and then everybody feels good again. The tantrum fulfilled its purpose—to make us feel angry or guilty so that he can get the toy back. This is just what we do when someone makes us angry. We try to make him angry or feel guilty so that he'll realize it is better to think like we do—because if not, we get angry, and nobody likes to see us angry.

If we analyze the situations in which we get angry, we can see how many times we are not able to make the other person angry or guilty—even worse, many times he does not even know we are angry! We can be in our house, really angry, thinking about it over and over, reinforcing the idea of anger, and the other person is at work or at home or at the cinema having a great time, without knowing about our anger.

Every time a child gets what he wants by making a scene or crying out loud, he reinforces the long-term neural connections linked to that specific behavior, and each time he repeats the scenario, the connections become stronger.

Throughout a lifetime, such an attitude can be strengthened more and more if a person gets what he is looking for through anger. The attitude can be reinforced with another person, parents, friends, etc.

Unconsciously, we think this is a good way to get something, so we make anger a way to get things. It doesn't matter what it is, it can be attention, things, or love. In time, however, we get to a point where we no longer have control over these behaviors.

To eradicate from our mind this way of thinking about getting angry as a way to get things for us, we need to have to have a new idea; the idea that the ego is the one that wants to control the way the others think, and make them think like we do.

As I said before we need to exercise this new idea for twenty-one days so that neural connections are formed in our brain and form a long-term relationship.

We can start with this exercise.

Every night for the next twenty-one days, before we go to sleep we will make a conscientious examination of all the times we got angry through the day.

Before you go to sleep, lie down in bed or sit comfortably, close your eyes and review the day, recalling every time you got upset or angry with someone else or with yourself. First remember generally, then specifically, with details of each situation. Approach it as if you were not you in the situation, rather cast yourself as an observer from outside. Doing it this way is of the utmost importance, as this will leave the emotions out of the examination, therefore not reinforcing the anger.

Ask yourself these questions. If you find it helpful, you may write down the answers.

- With whom was I angry?

- How did I feel?

- How did my body react?

- What did I say?

Now here is the most important part of the exercise:

Imagine that in the same circumstances you act differently. Imagine the same situation again, but because you now know that the other person is thinking differently than you, you will see the situation in a different way; this time you will see it without being angry.

This will help you realize that the other person has a different way of seeing the world than you do, that he has lived his life in different circumstances, which have led him to think in a different way. At this moment, we can understand he is not guilty of what we thought he was guilty of—and neither are we.

Create a clear picture in your mind of yourself at peace. See yourself in the same situation but at peace; you are at peace because now you know why you reacted the way you did and you also know why the other person thinks the way he does.

Consider the athlete who starts practicing the technique of a specific sport consciously. He keeps practicing until his mind is set, and after a while he no longer has to think about technique, unconsciously he makes the same move without thinking. In the same way, this will happen to us: after a while you will no longer need to do these exercises. You will act quietly and peacefully in the circumstances that previously made you angry.

At first this will be enough, and you will be reinforcing this idea in your mind. Then we'll try a couple of other exercises so that we can get to the peace we want and leave our anger behind.

"IF YOU HAVE TO CHOOSE BETWEEN BEING RIGHT AND FEELING GOOD, CHOOSE FEELING GOOD"

I once heard Dr. Wayne Dyer use this phrase, and since then it has made me change my way of looking at relationships with others.

All the wars that have taken place in the world have been fought because someone wanted to be right and fought for it, including killing others who didn't think his way and imposing his point of view for the "benefit" of the other country.

This does not happen just between nations or in lawsuits; it can happen in a conversation when we feel the need to impose our point of view. That's why most of us are not listening to the other person at all, we're thinking about what we're going to say next, and try to convince him to accept our point of view.

If you are determined to be "right," then be right about not needing to convince everyone about the way you think, or you will feel constantly unhappy.

When the ego can't impose its point of view, it feels miserable. Next time, the ego will look for new arguments in order to confront the point of view of others and then impose its own.

This way the ego defends itself is to become greater, to inflate itself when someone's view of us (or our thoughts or ideas) conflicts with the way we see those things. The ego in those situations feels the need to defend itself at any price, regardless of who made the comment, even if it means destroying a family relationship or even if it means we are going to feel unhappy or sad as a result.

If we are aware that it is the ego that wants to impose its way of seeing the world, we can change the way we look at those situations in the future and we'll have a different perception than the one we have now.

CHANGING YOUR PERCEPTION

Answer the following question:

Do you want to feel good?

Initially everybody responds, "Yes" so why don't we stop getting angry and feel good most of the time?

Well it's not quite that simple. At first, our ego plays a large part to make us mad. The ego does not care if we suffer; the most important thing in the world for the ego is to be right, even at the expense of our happiness or our health.

As I mentioned before, the ego has a terrible fear of dying (not the body, but the concept of its vulnerable self) and that leads it to defend its point of view at all costs. If someone has a different opinion than ours, even something as minor as the weather or the type of clothing you like, the ego immediately tells you to defend your opinion; and if you don't, you'll feel bad.

To the ego, every conversation is a battle that has to be won. The ego does not listen, it just want to put forward its opinions and then it feels alive—that's why we feel bad when someone expresses an opinion contrary to ours. When someone does not think the way we do—as in the expression of an opinion we disagree with—we become angry.

The ego wants to put its opinion forward at any price, even if it makes us mad. For the ego, our feeling bad is not important, what really is important is for it to be right.

Now, do you prefer to be right or to be happy?

The answer is simple, but the distinction is important: You want to be happy, but the ego wants you to be right.

The ego always wants to be right and defend what it has. That's why we feel the need to defend our point of view. The ego will do anything to make us believe it, it will even activate a feeling of discomfort and anger in our body in order to make us defend our opinion, and if we succeed in defending our opinion, the discomfort is likely to disappear and then we feel good again.

Usually, though, it's the opposite: we feel very bad after we get angry, even though we may have convinced others about our opinion. Once we have calmed down, we often feel bad about what we said or what we did. Generally fathers who have beaten their children for disobeying them feel very guilty for mistreating the people they love most in this world.

But the ego does not care about that, the ego only cares about being right and successfully defending its point of view. How you feel does not matter to the ego.

EVERYONE WHO UNDERSTANDS THIS DEEP WITHIN HIMSELF WILL HAVE THE GATES OF HEAVEN OPEN TO HIM

In other words, if you understand how the ego behaves deep within you, you will be able to detect when the ego is acting—and then the doors to peace and happiness will open for you.

Let's look at two situations, same facts, two different ways of listening to the ego.

SITUATION I

FIRST SCENARIO

Let's go back to the situation where a driver fails to yield the right of way. This time there are two cars, which are almost hit by the offending car.

In the first car a woman yells, blows the horn and gets really mad at the other driver. She comes home mad and shouts at her children. When her husband gets home she is still feeling mad; she tells him what happened on the street and relives the moment again in her mind, feeling the same anger she felt before.

Let's see what is happening with her ego:

First: A driver does not yield the right of way. The ego immediately activates feelings of discomfort and anger in order to make her understand that she "must" defend her point of view, to let others know that she is "right" and the other person is "wrong." She then obeys the ego and shouts at the other driver in order to make him see that he is wrong, letting him know she really knows the driver did something wrong.

Second: She comes home angry, not because someone else fouled up, but because she could not defend her point of view: after she insulted the driver, he shouted back at her, so she knew the other driver didn't understand he was wrong—and for the ego, this is the worst thing that can happen.

Therefore the ego feels attacked, feels even that it is dying, so it sends out feelings of discomfort and anger. The woman accordingly defends her point of view, but then failing to "convince" the other driver, she is driven by the ego to turn to others. So, she yells at her kids so that she can still be "right." This is always easier with someone who is more or less helpless and who respects and loves her.

Third: Now that she has made her point to her children, the ego has calmed down a bit but still feels bitter because it could not convince the other driver that he was wrong, so it waits for her husband to get home, then starts looking for approval about being right. If her husband tells her that she was in the right, then the ego will have succeeded about being "right" and the others "wrong."

Fourth: It doesn't end here. The ego remembers that the woman could not convince the other driver that he was "wrong" and therefore, as often as possible thereafter it uses similar circumstances to prove its "rightness." Every time someone does something "wrong" on the street, the ego triggers the same mechanism to enforce the woman's opinion and make her feel angry.

In our first scenario

Same situation—a car does not yield the right of way and almost hits two cars. In the first of these is the woman who got mad in our previous scenario; in the second car, there's woman who ignores the ego in such circumstances. She is living the same event at the same time—she even felt adrenaline running through her veins as her body perceived the danger of the situation.

She then crosses the intersection carefully and watches the other car driving off. She does not shout anything at him, but she thanks God for saving her from an accident. Then she turns to see if her children are okay, and tells them to thank God for keeping them from an accident and possibly going to the hospital.

That night, when her husband comes home, she tells him about the incident, telling him how lucky he is that his family is safe at home.

Without a doubt, the ego tried to make her upset in order to defend her point of view, but she was above the ego and knew in the depths of her being that she was very lucky that nothing bad happened to them.

When you are connected with your inner self, the ego loses control and cannot make us defend ourselves with our "right" point of view. But the most important thing is that this person knows the other person did something that was improper, which makes him a different thinker than her. She pays no attention to the ego and she doesn't get angry, because she knows we all think differently.

Almost anyone can accept the fact that we all think differently, but a lot of us don't easily accept the fact that although we all think differently, the other person *must* think, in certain circumstances, *just as I think*, because the ego tells me that I have the correct way of thinking.

Therefore if you accept the fact that your way of thinking is not necessary the right one, the times you get mad will decrease on time. If we believe this is true, then we will accept that that even though someone else thinks differently from the way we think, they are not wrong.

SITUATION II

Imagine a situation where a child plays with a camera and breaks it.

In our first scenario, the father is angry with the child because he did not respect his possessions. The camera was important to him and had cost him a lot of money.

The father reacts against his son; he spanks him and yells at him:

"How did you think playing with my camera was okay? Can't you see it is something that can be broken? I'm disappointed that you don't respect my things. Now you're grounded and you will not have that birthday gift you wanted so much; with that money I'm going to buy myself a new camera."

Why does the father get angry with the child?

He is mad because his son did not think like he did. The father knows that the camera is a valuable item, which can be easily broken if not handled carefully. He assumes the child sees things just as he does, which is indeed the correct way of looking at them: a camera can be easily broken if you play with it.

At that moment, the father and son relationship has been fractured.

In the second scenario, the boy's father gets upset, but he recognizes that the responsibility for taking care of the camera is not the child's. He also recognizes that the camera's value is only valid for him and not to his son, who only sees the camera as something to play with (until he is able to understand the value it represents for the adults). If the father hasn't let him know this, he does not have the right to punish him for the way he used the camera. He then talks with his son:

"Son, I'm upset that you broke the camera. I never told you it was so important to me, and now that it is broken, it is going to cost me money to replace it. Next time, please take extra care and do not play with my things so that this does not happen again."

It is possible that the father that punished his son feels guilty not because the camera is broken, but because he has hurt his son. This feeling can last years, and the son can be marked for his father reaction, not just physically, but mentally.

The father in the second scenario will not only have bad feelings for punishing his son, but he has reinforced in the child the idea that we can learn from our mistakes instead of feeling bad for making mistakes, he also reinforced a relationship based in trust instead of authority.

CHAPTER VIII

DISCUSSIONS

From the time we were children we faced others through discussions. If there was something we did not like, then we wanted to let others know that we did not like it, and we did so by getting angry.

Others also let us know they are angry with us when we upset them or do something they don't like.

We have to face discussions from an early age. When we are little we haven't yet learned to ask for things nicely, so if someone takes something away from us, we scream, cry, or hit them. This opens up a fantastic new world: we learn that in this world everything has a consequence—if we take a toy away from our little brother, he starts crying and yelling, and we notice that it is not only a reaction of losing the toy, but it is a reaction that we control. If we return the toy, then he stops crying, if we take it away again, he cries again. Through these experiences we learn that we can have power over others, power to make them react to our actions or words; we learn no push buttons.

We also learn that sometimes the power we have is not so funny, because with some children, if we take something away from them or say something that bothers or offends them, it makes them angry and they may react violently, hitting or biting us. We learn that this power is a double-edged sword that can bring painful consequences to us.

If I learn this as child, without adult intervention but only by our own experience, then I have no need to continue to experience this power to learn how to use it and I have no need to make someone else suffer so that I feel good.

But as parents, we strive to keep our children from suffering and will avoid this suffering whenever we can; this includes the times when we show them our opinion so they will not suffer in the future. We try to teach them about experiences that made us suffer so they can avoid them. We can only teach the world to our children in the way we perceive it, so we let them know what we believe is good and what we believe is wrong, but if we let them learn from their own experiences and let them make their own mistakes, they will see the world through their own eyes and not through ours.

In his book The New Child, Osho explains this by way of his own experience, thus teaching us that the child learns to see the world as it is and not what others see, for example, his own parents. To our Western way of seeing the world this teaching is radical and contrary to everything we have learned about the education of children, but if we take its essential message and use it to help us educate our children and let them learn from the consequences of their actions, it will keep them from suffering as they grow up and they can move toward the happiness we desire for them.

Although some of us did have a measure of freedom as children to learn from the consequences of our actions, most of us were under the influence of our parents, and we see the world largely through the filters that our parents, in their love for us, gave us so that we could avoid suffering. But that stopped the process of the power struggle with others.

For example, if we couldn't reach an agreement with our brother before our parents intervened, we did not complete the necessary process that would have shown us how the power we have to control the feelings of others can be dangerous. We were left with an incomplete understanding of the misuse of power, only learning that we can upset others if we do this or that to them, or if we say something that hurts them.

As adults, we want to continue using this power with others, and our attitude deepens over time with the ego reinforcing the idea of who it believes we are, what we have gained, and what we have now. When the ego feels threatened, it instantly remembers that power learned in childhood and uses it to avoid its own death, regardless of whether or not it makes *us* feel bad.

We cannot blame our own parents for educating ourselves that way, but this is the natural reaction of all parents, and most of the times it is the only way they knew how to educate us.

I'M ALWAYS RIGHT AND OTHERS ARE ALWAYS WRONG.

This is the prevailing thought of the ego. The ego always wants to be right and will do anything possible to have its way. The ego will do anything it can to make others think as it does.

Many people seem to want to talk about their problems, but most of the time people just want to be right. They're not seeking solutions to their problems; they just want to be right while others are wrong.

The next time you meet with your friends or family, take the opportunity to look beyond the conversations and see how everyone's egos want to convince others that they are right. When you are in a meeting, resist the temptation to convince others of your point of view, in fact try to speak as little as possible to be able to see reality as it is. You will begin to see how some people, when their advice is not taken, some others will try to convince others of the "rightness" of their views. Probably they will raise their voices in an effort to convince others of what they believe is right.

You do not need to be in an important conversation, it can be small talk; but in any conversation, the ego tries to convince others that it is right—even regarding something trivial.

Let's look at an example of this:

Patty: "A couple of days ago I had a terrible headache, I took two aspirins but it did not go away."

Laura: "At those times, Excedrin Extra is way better."

P: "But I always take a couple of aspirins."

L: "Aspirin? Aspirin is for a cold or a light headache, not for strong headaches."

P: "I believe Excedrin is too strong for me."

L: "But you just said you had a headache and aspirins did not work, so you should take Excedrin."

P: "Do you think Excedrin is the best?"

L: "I am sure if you take them next time you get a headache, it will disappear."

P: "Okay, I understand, but I am not convinced yet."

L: "Look, tomorrow I'll buy you some Excedrin, so next time you get a headache you take a couple."

At first it seems that Laura just wants to help Patty with her headaches, but if we look more carefully, Patty never asked Laura for advice about medications, she was just making conversation, perhaps looking for some compassion or empathy from Laura.

Laura's ego immediately felt threatened by her friend because she did not think like her—she thought aspirins were the best for headaches, but she was "wrong." The conversation then turned into a hidden battle of egos, each ego trying to convince the other that it was wrong.

If the conversation had started with Patty asking for advice about headache remedies, then the conversation might have been helpful, not a battle of egos.

If there had been several friends together, then the battle of egos probably would have multiplied, even though it started with something as simple as the mention of a headache. Each ego believes it is "right" and therefore it believes that the others are "wrong."

This happens frequently in conversation, but because we are immersed in it, we don't realize what's really happening. Instead of listening, we focus only on defending our ego. The answer here is to resist the ego's insistence on asserting its point of view and to listen as others give their points of view. As we listen, we may find an opportunity to offer our point of view—but we can offer it as *just what it is: our way of seeing the world.* In this way, we do not have to convince others that we are right and they are wrong.

This seems simple, and it is—but it is not easy. It is simple because it works, but it is not easy because we live in a society that taught us to defend our point of view, and defending our thoughts is something we have done since childhood. We feel that if we do not defend our point of view, we are weak, when in reality the opposite is true: it takes more courage not to defend your point of view than to defend it.

The next time you give your opinion about an issue and others do not agree with you, stop talking and resist the need you will feel to defend your point of view. You may feel a discomfort in the stomach or in the chest; this is the ego sending signals to your body to remind you that you need to defend yourself at all costs. In these moments, it is not so easy to keep quiet.

Inside of you, the ego feels it is dying, so it sends signals of discomfort to the body, telling you to defend yourself at all costs, making you think that if you "win" this conversation, the discomfort will disappear and you will feel good again.

But what if you resist this need to defend your point of view?

NOTHING WILL HAPPEN

If you resist, you've advanced a long way in the process of working with the ego—you've learned to control one of the greatest challenges of the ego and you will have much more productive conversations. When you're in the midst of discussions you will not feel threatened and you can really see these conversations just as they are, not as the ego says they are, and you will not feel the need to defend your point of view.

BUT SOMETIMES IT IS WORTH IT TO DEFEND YOUR POINT OF VIEW

When I advise you to resist the temptation to defend your point of view, I do not mean that you should live passively and let others make life decisions for you. I am only stressing that when the ego wants to defend itself, you should resist this temptation and not defend your point of view. The key to doing this is to know when the ego is talking.

When you are sure your heart, and not your ego, is telling you to defend your point of view, you can be sure it is worth it.

If, for example, your teenager wants to go out at night and you know that's not the best thing for him, by all means defend your point of view.

If your project at work is the one that will best help the company, defend your opinion.

If you see abuses against another human being, then of course you should defend your opinion.

This happens to me with my children. When I give them an instruction and they question it, my first impulse is to defend my instruction. Then I stop and think it over, and if it is something I am sure is best for them, then it has to be done. For example, if they have to go to school but they don't want to get out of bed, there's no choice—they get up and go. But in other circumstances during the day if I analyze it and believe they can be right and my instruction can be changed without any damage, then I change it.

Once when my wife was away for the weekend, I told my two sons to take a shower and then have dinner. My reasoning was that while they were taking a shower, I would fix dinner. But they asked me if they could do it the other way around, giving me their own reasons: they said they preferred to eat first so they could watch TV while I made dinner for them; they would have dinner quickly, and I would have time to fill the tub, then they would take a bath and go to bed warmer (warmer than the other way).

At first I was going to defend my point of view. I had already given an instruction and expected it would be followed because I am their father. Fortunately, I resisted the temptation to defend my statement and recognized that they had a valid point of view. It did not affect their bedtime, and it turned out to be better for them than my plan.

I didn't lose my authority as a parent, because at the end they took a bath and had dinner; instead, they gained self-esteem as they realized that they could give their opinion without being seen as wrong all the time. This happens to all parents: We listen to ego rather than listening to our children's thoughts.

MOST OF THE PEOPLE YOU'RE FIGHTING WITH JUST WANT TO BE RIGHT

When someone begins arguing with you, chances are he really does not want to solve anything, he just wants to be right and feel that you are wrong.

Lots of people will tell you their problems, but most of the time people just want to be right without really seeking solutions to their problems. This is why once you get into an argument, it is very difficult to come to an agreement, because if all that is happening is a clash of egos, all the egos want is to be right, no matter how it makes you feel.

In a couple's relationship, egos can be present in everyday talk (as in this example), and even more present in deeper discussions, like this:

"Why didn't you take out the garbage?"

"I've been busy, besides I just came from work and I don't feel like doing housework."

"But the garbage has been there for more than three days."

"I know, but I haven't had time to do it."

"It is already starting to smell—it could even make us sick."

49

"I do not want to do it right now, if you wait until tomorrow I'll do it. If not, you can take it out yourself."

"We agreed it was your responsibility to take out the trash, not mine."

"Yeah, but we didn't agree to do it whenever you wanted."

This conversation began with something trivial—taking out the trash— then escalated to a war of egos where neither side would give up. This only hurts a relationship. Because neither person's ego was willing to give up, neither of them was willing to recognize that the other was right. Because egos were fighting, there was no chance of finding a solution.

If we just look at the conversation's surface, we see that the wife did not want to take out the garbage—that was her husband's job, not hers. But if we look more closely, we see that mostly she wanted to be right and let his husband know that he was wrong.

Why didn't you take out the garbage?

She started the conversation with "why" and in that moment she made it a claim—it is a claim, because a question that starts with a "why" has no satisfactory answer. Questions starting with "why" invite the one being questioned to make excuses or to be defensive, not to solve a conflict.

Questions beginning with "why" are usually asked by people who only want their ego to be justified, they don't want a solution.

If the same conversation had started this way, things would have been different:

"Can you please take the garbage out today before it starts to smell?"

This is a request, which has the objective of getting things done and does not seek to make the other person feel bad just because he failed to do something.

She also could have let her husband know the way she was feeling:

"When I come home and see the garbage bags still inside the house, I feel very bad. Can I ask you to please take it out in the morning before you go?"

This is a request that is looking to get things done, and it also shares with her husband how she feels about this—but without wanting to make him feel bad. Her way of putting it is intended to let him know that when he doesn't take the garbage out, as agreed, she feels bad, and he can help her not feel that way by cooperating.

But be careful when you express your feelings, because they can turn into a claim:

"I hate it when you don't take the trash out in the morning."

This way, it is again a claim: she is definitely angry. She is not thinking about how to ask him to help but just asking for an argument. It is clear that it is her ego trying to make her husband feel bad. And even though it seems she is letting him know how she feels, she is doing it as a claim that is designed to make her husband become defensive and to get into a "discussion" which will be filled with excuses and efforts to determine which of them is "right."

Although in the end she might get him to take out the garbage, what she also will have achieved is making him angry and resentful: the next time he fails to take out the garbage, he will remember this argument and the relationship then becomes weak and they start losing respect for each other.

The key is the way in which things are asked, and whether you really want a solution or just want to make someone feel bad.

Of course this sounds very simple to read about, quietly and without feelings involved, but in reality you are going to be angry and you will likely make unfair claims on others.

So far, what is important is we recognize when we made a claim or when we asked things in order to get them done—even though we find it out after the fact.

When we know the difference, before we speak we can restructure our words to make a request instead of a claim. Doing this is taking a step toward a life free of anger. We can be really angry at any given moment, but that does not mean we are going to make the other person feel bad and spoil our chances of getting things done. It means you can feel anger and yet have the sense to get what you want. Chances are, when you recognize the difference between a claim and a request, a similar situation will not make you angry again.

It means that we are free to choose our words and our actions even when we are upset. We do not have to get carried away by ego instinctively, but rather have a choice to decide how we will respond to anger.

CHAPTER IX

WHY DO WE GET MAD
WITH OURSELVES?

It is a huge irony, but we humans get angry with ourselves.

We have a hard time forgiving ourselves, sometimes even a harder time than when we try to forgive others.

To understand why we get angry with ourselves, we first have to take into account two aspects of this type of anger.

If we get angry with ourselves, we have to accept the existence of another being within us—but why? Because one being disagrees with what "the other one" did or said. But if there is only one person and not two inside of us, we could not disagree with ourselves.

If we recognize we have another being inside of us, or another entity called the ego, then which one is real? It is us: the being that is connected with God all the time and is an infinite and eternal being. It is real and that is what we are, that essence of God.

If we are part of God, then this being cannot be angry. The being that we are is, in essence, love, and this love is way beyond anger.

If this is true and this being is only love, then the being that gets angry is the ego.

Anger is easy to understand when we get angry with someone else, but when we get angry with ourselves, then it is a bit more complicated, because in order to work it out logically, we have to accept the idea that there are two different beings inside of us.

If we accept this, then it seems we need to accept that we have a little bit of insanity in us. But isn't it a kind of madness—getting mad with ourselves? We get angry with ourselves for something we did, for something that we are responsible for, nobody else did it for us, we did it alone, and in that moment we agreed to do it.

Getting mad with ourselves is the ego acting at its best; one of the most-used tools of the ego is blame. In order to be angry with ourselves, the ego uses guilt, and this keeps us apart from reality and from the moment, and away from the knowledge that we are all part of God.

If we are angry with ourselves or have resentment toward ourselves, then we are accepting the idea that we are not part of God, because God is perfect and if we make mistakes and do bad things, then we cannot be part of God. This is where the ego achieves its goal, which is to take us away from God and away from reality as it is. It wants to make us believe that we are "bad" in order to separate us from our real being.

Most of the times we get mad during the day are with ourselves. Sometimes we do not like the way we look or don't like our body. We get mad if we are late; we don't like that we are short, or fat, or skinny; we believe we are not beautiful enough for others, we believe we are not good enough, period, and all of these things make us mad with ourselves.

This is one of life's greatest ironies, that we live our lives angry about what we are, or angry about what we are not. This is one of the ego's best tricks, its principal act of magic, to make us believe we are imperfect and that we need to get angry for every mistake we make. The ego succeeds in distracting us from the present moment, —*which is the only thing that is real.*

Recognizing this is one of the greatest advances on the path to eradicating the ego in us.

When we repress or blame ourselves, we obstruct the natural learning process—that of learning from our mistakes.

When we are young, we learn by imitation, but we also learn by our mistakes. We learned to walk after we fell down many times, but that didn't bother us, because every time we fell, we learned something. Every mistake was a step toward achieving our goal, so that after so many mistakes, we finally learned to walk. Then after we learned to walk, we felt down again many times, but that did not stop us from walking. We kept walking, and never doubted that we would get to our goal.

This process, which is natural in human beings (and also in animals), is something we start to lose as we begin to pay attention to others' opinions—our parents, friends, brothers and sisters, and teachers. Most of these opinions have a good intention, but as we take them as true, they limit us. Eventually we learn to reprimand ourselves, to condemn many of our own actions. This was enhanced when others didn't like what we did, especially when our parents, teachers, and friends got mad because of our behavior.

These are the external causes of our anger, the causes we believed made us mad with ourselves, but the reality is that the ego is the one that taught us to repress our attitudes. The ego believes that we are what we have and what others think of us, but if we lose this good image others have of us, the ego feels it is in danger; that is why it taught us to repress ourselves—to toe the line—in order to gain the acceptance of others, but at the same time eliminating or decreasing our acceptance of ourselves.

And if ego is the other "being" inside of us which is making us mad, then:

THE ONLY REASON IN THE WORLD YOU GET MAD IS BECAUSE YOU THINK YOU ARE RIGHT, AND THE OTHER PERSON IS WRONG.

This can be understood only if we accept the fact that while the ego lives inside us, *the ego is not us but is a false self.*

If we understand this, we will treat ourselves kindly and let go of the temptation to blame or feel hatred for ourselves.

Dr. Bob Rotella, a highly esteemed sports psychologist, tells us that in the game of golf, the golfer's hardest critic is himself. He says that nobody would pay a caddy to treat them badly, to scream at them and criticize every shot for not being perfect, throwing away the clubs each time they don't hit a shot well; but we treat ourselves like that all the time.

On a golf course you can see this all the time: adult players throwing tantrums, throwing clubs, swearing, saying things to themselves that nobody else would dare to say to them. And yet we are supposed to be grownups!

Dr. Rotella says these attitudes are harmful to a golfer's optimum performance. Every time we do this kind of thing, we reinforce the idea of a bad shot instead of reinforcing the idea of a good shot. In golf, the reaction to a bad shot is more noticeable than the reaction to a shot good; this means we are reinforcing the idea that we only make bad shots on the course.

But the most important thing Dr. Rotella tells us is this: when you make a bad shot, forget it and focus only on the shot you have now, the shot you have at this moment, not the one you had in the past. He tells us to be present all the time, because what most affects the result is not the bad shot and thinking about the past, but the present moment, when you are about to make the shot.

An ancient Zen legend says:

There were once two monks studying Zen walking along by a river, when they saw a woman who could not cross the river.

One of them, seeing her concern, picked her up and helped her cross the river.

But Zen monks are not allowed to touch a woman in any way, so the other monk, seeing what his partner had done, was bothered and got mad because the other monk broke the rules.

Both monks continued their journey, but the second monk couldn't stop thinking about his friend's mistake.

They reached the monastery at dawn, and the monk who had been thinking about the incident could not contain himself any longer, and he said to the other monk:

"What you did at the river was wrong! Although that woman needed help, you know we are not permitted to touch women, but you did it anyway."

The other monk calmly replied:

"My dear friend, I carried the woman across the river hours ago; but you are still carrying her."

The monk who helped the woman was living in the present, so there was no place for repression. The other monk was in the past, putting blame on the other monk for his "mistake." The lesson of the story is to be PRESENT; because in the present there is no place for anger.

If we analyze our anger in detail, we realize that when we get angry during the day, it is with ourselves, or as we said before: the ego makes us angry with ourselves in order to survive.

If we could stop getting angry with ourselves, we would not be angry that often during the day.

To quit getting angry with ourselves is a process, which begins by recognizing this anger, continues with accepting it, and at the end it disappears.

To help us recognize our self-anger, I recommend making a list of our anger at the end of the day. It is easy for us to forget the angers we felt during a day, but as we become more aware of our angers, we will start writing more and more:

1. With whom did I get mad?

2. What did the other person do to make me mad? What did the other person do that I believed was wrong?

3. Could I have done something differently so that this might not have happened?

4. Was I upset with myself?

5. What will I do the next time this happens to me?

The first question starts the process.

The second question helps us see the situation clearly.

The third question helps us answer the fourth: if my answer to no. 3 is "yes," then I am mad at myself.

And even if we get angry with someone else, try to find out if we are really angry with *ourselves* for something we did or said or failed to do which made the other person act in a certain way or say something that made us mad.

Number five is not only a question; it is the first step towards a real change inside of us.

Let's see it in a real-life situation:

Laura finds out at the end of the day that her daughter didn't do her homework, and now it's too late to do it because she has to go to bed so that she can be alert the next day.

Laura yells at her daughter, telling her that it is her responsibility (her fault) because she played all afternoon instead of doing the homework.

Her daughter goes to bed scolded, and with her homework uncompleted.

So if Laura takes her anger exam at night, it might look like this:

1. With whom did I get mad?

I GOT MAD AT MY DAUGHTER.

2. What did the other person do to make me mad? What did the other do that I believed was wrong?

SHE DIDN'T DO HER HOMEWORK BECAUSE SHE WAS PLAYING IN THE AFTERNOON.

3. Could I have done something differently so that this might not have happened?

YES, I COULD HAVE REMINDED HER ABOUT THE HOMEWORK WHEN SHE GOT FROM SCHOOL.

4. Was I upset with myself?

YES, I WAS UPSET WITH MYSELF BECAUSE I DIDN'T REMIND HER ABOUT HER HOMEWORK, AND I KNOW THAT WHEN SHE STARTS PLAYING, SHE DOESN'T THINK ABOUT HER HOMEWORK.

5. What will I do the next time this happens to me?

I'LL TALK TO MY DAUGHTER AND TELL HER HOW IMPORTANT IT IS TO DO HER HOMEWORK, BUT MORE IMPORTANTLY, EACH DAY I WILL MAKE A SCHEDULE FOR HER HOMEWORK AND MAKE SURE SHE FINISHES BEFORE SHE GOES OUT TO PLAY.

Laura was very angry, but actually she was angry because she was feeling guilty, thinking her daughter would have done the homework if Laura had reminded her about it. Then she wouldn't have gotten mad at her daughter.

The reaction was against her daughter, but she really wasn't forgiving herself for the guilt she felt her daughter had to suffer the next day as a consequence of not doing the homework.

This is pure learning. If we know we can act differently in a situation like this, then we are prepared to respond rather than react; with each new experience, we can analyze an array of possible behaviors at our disposal, and act according to what is really happening.

Learning to act rather than react is very important. It is possible that we will still get mad in the same situation in the future instead of taking the action we had planned. But these are not failures, they are a part of learning; as we learn more and more each time, we strengthen the idea. In time, our reactiveness will dissipate, and we will act instead of reacting unconsciously.

As we come to realize that we actually get mad at ourselves rather than with others, our reactions will be different than before we knew this—and every day it will be a little easier.

CHAPTER X

BLAME

The easiest way I know to show you what I really think about guilt is with a story:

THE BLAME TRICK

Once upon a time, in the beginning of times, there was a small village, away by itself up in the mountains.

It was in a beautiful landscape full of rivers, lakes, and forests, and even the animals lived in harmony with nature and man.

The village people lived in peace with themselves and with others. Everyone had a different task and each task was as important as the others; all performed their duties with enthusiasm and everyone served the community.

At the end of the work day, all the people gathered on the shore of the lake, waiting for something wonderful that happened every day just before sunset: God appeared on the lake and talked with the villagers.

They talked about how they lived in the day; their good moments, their not-so-good moments, and God listened to everyone and gave advice to those who asked for it.

When God finished talking and giving advice, he left them with wise words to ponder for a while.

And as we all know, everyone who listens to God every day becomes wiser every day and lives life in harmony. So this was a wise village and its inhabitants lived in harmony.

Although they lived in happiness, things didn't always work perfectly. But when something didn't work as planned, God was always there to talk to them and show them the answers to their questions.

But one day a wizard who had been expelled from another town came to the village. He had been expelled because he had been using his magic only to his own benefit, without caring if he hurt others. This magician was known as Ego.

No one from outside had ever come to this village, but the magician, using his magic, found it.

At first people did not know what to do. He was the first foreign visitor, but as they were good people, Ego was received as one of them; they gave him a home and food.

The magician was used to being heard, talking and convincing others to his point of view. He was full of pride and envy, and because of this, he began to talk in public in the afternoons. No one listened; everyone preferred to listen to God. This really made the wizard mad, so he continued to do everything possible in order to be heard.

Getting people to listen to him turned out to be harder than he thought. The magician tried various spells, some intended to mesmerize the people. But they were so close to God that spells lasted only a moment, then lost their power over them.

The magician looked in all his books and made all of the most sophisticated spells, but none worked.

Finally he came to the conclusion that the only way people would listen to him was if they stopped listening to God, so he invented a spell to stop the villagers from listening to God. It took him months, but when he finally got it, he called this powerful spell *blame*.

This spell was powerful; the way it worked was that every time someone made a mistake, the spell would take effect and would blame someone else for the mistake. Instead of taking full responsibility for the mistake, and learning from it, the villagers started to blame others, therefore they passed the guilt for having made a mistake on to someone else.

Every day more people began listening to the magician; his opinion became important to many people, more and more people called him for advice, taking his opinion as their own. The magician began to have power over the people, and suddenly became the highest authority in the village.

Eventually, people stopped going to talk to God and stopped asking God for advice. It became easier to blame someone instead of trying to solve his or her problems themselves. Harmony in the village changed to conflict. There were problems among neighbors, and some even started having fights within families.

So finally, one day God went to the lake as usual, but there was no one to talk to. He waited and waited, but nobody came, but God loved the villagers so much that he continued going to the lake day after day, hoping to find someone to talk to.

Time passed and the idea of talking to God was forgotten, it became nothing more than a beautiful story to remember; people no longer had time to talk with God.

Then one day something mysterious happened: A young carpenter who lived in the village, who was thinking about a big problem and was wondering who to blame for it, happened to arrive at the lake. He saw a child by the lake and began walking toward him. As he got closer, he realized that the child alone, but talking, and he noticed that the child was really happy—talking to no one. This caught his attention even more, and he asked the child:

"Whom are you talking to?"

The boy was surprised by the question. He answered:

"I'm talking with God. Can't you see him? He is over there."

The carpenter looked but he didn't see anybody.

While the carpenter was looking around, the child kept talking:

"God comes here to the lake every day, and I come here and talk to him. He listens to me and gives me advice if I ask for it."

The carpenter then remembered that when he was a child he used to come with his parents to the lake every afternoon, and he remembered that he used to see God and talk to him. At that moment, tears fell from his eyes, and he began to feel a deep sorrow, because he realized he could not see God anymore, he couldn't even hear God anymore, because he was listening to ego instead.

And this is how the ego invented blame, so that we wouldn't listen to God but instead listen to the ego.

The end.

Blame is nothing but a shield so we don't take responsibility for our actions.

We are used to blaming everything: We blame the weather, we blame the financial situation, we blame others, we blame the traffic, we blame the government, and we even blame ourselves.

Guilt is one of the lowest energies that exist. We feel guilty when our life energy is low; to others we project a poor image of ourselves, and our actions correspond to that energy.

It is the same when we blame others. When we blame someone else, we keep that low energy in us, even though we believe we passed away to someone else, in reality most of the times we blame someone else, that person doesn't even know about it, the situation that bothered us remains static. Blaming others is not the solution.

The weather doesn't care if the whole city blames it, or if you arrive to work late because of it. The president doesn't know you are upset because of something he said last month. The government almost never knows what we are saying about it. We often blame the government for our economic situation, but most of the time governments can't or won't do anything about it.

Passing the blame to others and refusing to take responsibility for our actions is something we learned when we were young. But now that we are talking about learning to blame, I want to tell you I do not blame your parents or mine; they did the best they could, the best they knew at that time. I'm not blaming, I'm just stating a fact to help you realize that this is learned, not something that was already in you before you were born.

But now that you know this, it is your responsibility to educate your children in a better way; educate them with awareness. Teach your children to learn differently than the way you learned. Learn how to teach your children to assume responsibility for every action they take—and without anger or raising your voice or punishing them; without blame.

We learn this first listening to our parents complains. They often blamed others for what happened in their lives—the government, their relatives, their bosses.

When we were spanked, we learned that when we did something others didn't like, we would suffer a painful punishment, so we learned to find ways to avoid suffering. The easiest thing we learned was to blame others, that way we would not have to take responsibility for our actions and not suffer punishment.

If we beat our brother, we would be punished. The next time, we would have learned from the previous punishment, so instead of taking the chance of getting punished again, we would find a way to blame someone else—so we told our parents that our brother had bothered us first.

If we got a C instead of a B or an A, we would try to blame the teacher, saying that he gave us a low grade because he didn't like us.

If we got sick, our parents (along with us) would blame the weather instead of taking responsibility, because we had forgotten to wear a jacket. That way, however, we didn't learn that next time we should bring a jacket with us.

Every time we make an excuse, we are using blame. We are used to blaming someone or something else, we have been practicing for years and we have become experts at it. We use blame in relationships, at school, at work, and at home.

The excuses are the ego's invention: the ego sees danger all the time, it believes that I am what I have, what I have achieved, and what I will be, but mostly it highly regards what others think of me, because what others think of me confirms what I think of myself. The ego believes that I *am* the good opinion others have of me, and if I do something that changes that view, the ego seeks to blame something or someone else so that my opinion of myself does not change; if someone else is "guilty" then I will remain the same as before. This is what the ego wants us to think.

We do not realize how many times we blame others and the number of excuses that we have to find in a day to put aside-taking responsibility for our actions.

When we complain, we are blaming without knowing it.

The other day I went to renew my driver's license. When I arrived I found that there were a lot of people ahead of me and that I'd have to wait for perhaps a couple of hours, so I left; as I was on my way out I realized there were discounts if the fee was paid by the end of the month.

When I got home I told my wife about it. I said I could not renew the license because of all the people that had arrived before me. I added that it was the government's fault because there were offering discounts in the month.

Without knowing it, I was blaming the government for giving discounts and I was also blaming all the people that had arrived there earlier than me.

When I saw that I was blaming others, I realized that I was actually upset with myself because I didn't go the previous month to renew it, I let the time pass by and now I could not wait until next month, because my license would expire this month. I was avoiding my responsibility for my own actions, would have been simply accepting that I had two choices, staying on line and losing a couple of hours, or returning the next day a little earlier.

I did return earlier the next day, I was among the first in line, and I renewed the license in half an hour.

I was blaming others so others wouldn't see that I had made a mistake and wouldn't change their good opinion about me.

We do so many of these things unconsciously, it is not easy to discover the real reason that we blame, but there are ways to help us find out:

I suggest that if you are already doing your anger list at night, you add excuses and blame:

1. Who did I blame?

2. Why did I blame him or her?

3. Could I have done something differently?

4. Did I blame myself?

5. What will I do next time this happens to me?

If I apply these questions to my trip to the motor vehicle department, I get this result:

1. Who did I blame?

I BLAMED THE GOVERNMENT AND THE PEOPLE WHO ARRIVED BEFORE ME.

2. Why did I blame him or her?

BECAUSE RENEWING THE LICENSE WOULD TAKE MORE TIME THAN I HAD PLANNED FOR.

3. Could I have done something differently?

YES, I COULD HAVE GONE A MONTH BEFORE.

4. Did I blame myself?

YES, I DID.

5. What will I do next time this happens to me?

A COUPLE OF MONTHS BEFORE MY LICENSE EXPIRES; I WILL GO TO RENEW IT. IF THERE ARE DISCOUNTS, THEN I WILL HAVE ANOTHER MONTH.

Using these simple questions, we can easily determine how many times we blamed others—and ourselves—during the day. We will realize that we make ourselves feel badly; we will accept that we are the cruelest judges of ourselves because we blame ourselves so many times during the day.

If we feel bad for something we did, it is because we have blamed ourselves, probably without even noticing it. The one that blamed us is really the ego, which blames in order to survive. Let's try to remember that the ego does not care if you feel good or bad, all it wants is to live.

If we start by knowing that the ego is not real, and that there can't be two people in us—one real and the other not real—then we will see that everything the ego says isn't real either.

By accepting this we can come to realize that every time we feel guilty, it is not real, it is just our ego trying to survive.

This doesn't mean we will not learn from our mistakes; quite the opposite: we are really seeking to learn from our mistakes and to correct them without feeling guilty.

If we trade the process of blaming for the process of learning we will feel much better, because when we learn something, we have a feeling of triumph, a feeling opposite to the feeling of guilt. When we feel guilty, we feel bad, which stops the learning process; instead of moving forward we move backward. We are supposed to grow with every mistake we make in our lives.

When we learn from our mistakes, we resume the process of learning we had begun when we were little, when we enjoyed the greatest achievements of our lives, such as walking. Imagine how big that achievement was! Or when we learned hundreds of words, verbs, rules of grammar so we could talk, read, and write. When we could tell others all that we wanted, these were some of the most important achievements in our lives. We learned from our falls and our mistakes, but we didn't let our mistakes stop us and we never felt guilty. Far from it—we felt great when we learned to walk. We can take back this learning process now and learn to grow with our mistakes, taking full responsibility for our actions and ourselves.

Blame dissolves when we comprehend this:

EVERYTHING HAPPENS FOR MY OWN SAKE.

This concept can be one of the most powerful of all. When we comprehend it, we don't have the need to be mad or blame. When we do it we open the doors of a new life, a life in purpose.

Many times we keep staring at the closed window, blaming others, and sometimes blaming God. We focus so much on that window that we can't see the huge open door that God opened for us.

When we understand this we will have a life where worries turn into opportunities, where problems are only signs on the road, telling us there is something better coming soon. When we do this we recognize there is something larger than us, that we are part of a supreme order; an order where everything has a reason to be, and that everything is for my own good.

Jesus said Faith moves mountains. Jesus wasn't talking exclusively about accepting God's existence; He was also talking about knowing in every moment God has always something good for me.

CHAPTER XI

LISTEN

There is a reason because we have two ears and one mouth so we can listen twice as much as we speak.

Epictecus

One of the simplest techniques to stop getting angry when someone speaks to you is to *listen, but to listen carefully.*

This is also simple, but not easy.

When we are in a conversation, what happens frequently is that we aren't really listening (although we believe we are); we are hearing some of the ideas the speaker is offering, but we are also making judgments about what we are hearing and looking for ways to defend our point of view regarding what we are hearing.

This behavior is also unconscious until we know better, but even when we know it, it isn't that simple to change.

But what if instead of listening to our own opinions and thoughts we really listened to the other person? What if we listened to the other person from the heart?

If we listen from the heart, we will feel empathy with the other person; we may not agree with what the other thinks or how he sees the situation at the time, but we will have the empathy to understand it and to understand the reasoning behind his thoughts. We will connect with this person, because we will have heard him from the heart.

If we listen with our heart, we will put aside the anger that is hidden in many of our conversations, an anger that almost goes unnoticed because we have become used to it. Because we have years of living with it every day, in every conversation we have, it is so subtle that we do not realize it anymore.

But it is a fact: every time we do not agree with someone else's comments and our ego tells us to defend our point of view, there is an anger which we are usually not aware of. But this anger seems to be a part of all the talks we have.

Because this is a very subtle anger and not easily perceived, once we realize we have it, the easy way to eradicate it is by listening to the other from the heart; without judging.

The next time you're in a meeting with friends, become aware of the thoughts you have on the conversation (other than what they say) and realize what goes through your head when you are listening to others.

When you have a thought, stop thinking and try to see if you are judging the other person for what he says. It is possible that you will begin judging him for what he did, or for what you think he could have done differently; maybe you think what he did was wrong or that you could have done it better. Look at the judgments that pop into your head.

Sometimes the judgments you have in your mind seem to want to help the other person; but in the end, judgments always want the ego to be right.

Let me give you an experience I had, that helped me realize this:

Friend: "I am starting to have a headache; I think I'm getting sick."

Me: (my inner dialogue): "He is starting to talk again about his illnesses. Why doesn't he understand that the more he talks about sickness, the sicker he will be?"

My judgments were based on my past experiences: when my friend was talking, I started to remember that several times before I had heard him talking about his diseases, and he did seem to get sick more than most people.

I was also judging that he was wrong for talking so much about his illness and that I was right because I did not. So I was not listening to him from the heart, I was only listening to my thoughts; I was busy making judgments based on my past experiences and not paying attention to what my friend was trying to tell me at that moment.

Often, when people tell you about their problems, they are not looking for advice or assistance; they are only looking for empathy. They want to be heard, even though you may not share their ideas. Remember the example of the friend who had a headache, and the other was trying to convince to take the medicine she believed was the best, she didn't listen to her friend, she was just focusing on her thoughts, on her own ideas of right and wrong, she was also busy trying to convince her friend she was right and the friend wrong.

This is why many people feel better when they tell their problems to someone else. In many cases, people who go into therapy start to feel better as soon as they begin telling the therapist their problems, and the therapist often just listens and guides the patient, who will himself find the needed solution.

Finding the solution ourselves is much more powerful than when someone else gives us advice or provides an answer. When someone gives us advice, we may feel that they are correcting us instead of trying to help us.

When we understand this, we will stop giving unsolicited advice to those who tell us their problems. We will also stop telling others that we have problems that are similar to, or even worse than, the ones they're telling us about.

But it is human nature to give advice and to talk about our problems, and this is another way the ego operates in order to protect itself. The ego tries to get others to have pity on us, or to take our thoughts as valid, in order to feel important. The ego does not listen; it only wants to be recognized. It has plenty of ways to boost the idea of who you are, what you have, and what others think about you.

One way to stop this ego-invented need is to become aware of the emotions we feel when we are listening to others:

How do I feel?

Am I feeling tension?

Where am I feeling the tension?

At first, it isn't easy to perceive this. We are not used to being aware of our emotions. Most of the time we are not aware of them, but that doesn't mean we don't feel them. We may feel badly, but without being able to identify where we feel the discomfort.

People usually feel emotions in the stomach, the chest, the heart, the head, and the neck.

By becoming aware of our emotions, we stop the ego's impulse to control what we are thinking and we begin to hear only what others are telling us.

Another technique that can help us listen to others is to ask them questions, using the their same terms. This is called establishing a rapport:

"Are you saying that you were angry with your child because he left his clothes on the floor?"

"You felt bad because your friend didn't call you on your birthday?"

This is a great way to help you keep your mind away from your own stories and focused on the speaker. It also helps you understand the feelings the other person is expressing.

Listening is an art, but with practice you can make it a habit in your everyday conversations and eventually you could stop feeling that urge to convince other about your point of view.

CHAPTER XII

EDUCATE CHILDREN WITHOUT GETTING MAD

An adult gets mad during the day most of the times in two places: at work and at home.

At home we get angry with our husband or wife, and with our children.

We are at the same level when we get mad at our husband or wife because we are adults and together by mutual agreement. Each has the power to end that relationship and leave—as happens in many marriages.

But with children it is completely different. They did not choose to live with us, they are smaller than we are and cannot decide to leave us and go live with some other adults.

With children we have an explicit authority that gives us power over them, a power that is misunderstood most of the time because we confuse the power with the authority.

Power can be abused, but authority is more likely to be fair.

When we abuse our power by beating our kids, shouting at them, or hurting them emotionally, we negatively affect their self-esteem, but more important, we affect their hearts.

When I talk about hurting them, I am not talking about those parents who abuse their children so much that they end up in jail because of it. I am talking about loving parents that get desperate at moments because their children don't listen to them or misbehave. They yell at them or spank them in order to correct them, not realizing that both are abuses of authority.

Imagine that you arrive at work one morning prepared to give your monthly report. Your boss takes a look at it and says:

"You're useless! You don't know how to make a report; I don't know why you are still at this company! Why are you so useless? Maybe what you really need is some punishment; maybe I shouldn't pay you this month."

Hard to imagine, isn't it? If you had a boss who was constantly screaming at you and humiliating you, you would probably end quitting your job.

This is what happens to our children when we shout at them and beat them: they feel humiliated and worthless. But as we said above, it is not within their power to leave home. They love us, and that's even worse for them since their most loved person is the one who humiliates them and hits them; what can they expect from a person who does *not* love them?

When we get angry with our children because they did something we regard as bad, we react in the way that we learned to react from experiences with our own parents.

One of the most common reactions we have when disciplining our children is to yell at them, punish them, or beat them in order "to teach them a lesson."

When the "fault" is not serious, we may only reprimand them, but most of the time we ask "why" in order to make them feel bad

"Why did you leave toys on the floor of your room?"

If the child honestly answered this question, we would probably get even angrier:

"I left them there because I went to play outside with my brother."

But we do not want an answer to our question, we just want to make them feel bad and to let them know that we are right and they are wrong.

We know from our previous discussion that "why" questions are meant to hurt somebody; they are not tools to facilitate a discussion but are instead a way to establish that we are right and the other person is wrong. We use these questions all the time:

"Why are you so lazy?"

"Why did you get these bad grades?"

"Why are you so late?"

"Why didn't you finish your homework?"

"Why did you drop that glass?"

We use all these questions, and many more, to make our children feel bad, but as we said earlier, we do so because we didn't know they were meant to hurt. We learned from our parents, who also didn't know this, so they kept asking us "why" questions when we were kids.

There are better ways to let our children know they did something that bothered us:

- "It bothers me when you leave your toys on the floor; please pick them up before you have dinner."

- "When you keep getting low grades, I get the impression you are not spending enough time studying. What are you going to do next time?"

- "It worries me when you get home late. Next time you need to get home at the time we agreed on."

- "You didn't finish your homework because you were doing other things; what are going to do to finish it?"

- "It bothers me to see a dirty table. Next time, can you pay better attention? This time, please clean the table."

Although some of these phrases are used with authority, all of them are meant to solve something or to facilitate better conduct in the future.

Using this kind of language instead of reprimands does not guarantee us that next time the same thing will not happen, in fact it is likely that the same behavior will occur in the future—and we will need to act as we did this time, until our kids understand. But if we fall again into reprimands and the "why" questions, we will just be going backwards.

It is even more important, when the same behavior keeps showing, that we remember to use our new skills. It may take a long time, but it will be worth it. We will achieve not only the eradication of the behavior that bothered us, but also will have increased our children's self-esteem as well as their trust toward us.

Although I can't absolutely guarantee results by using this method, I can assure you that by doing so you will be treating your child as another being like you, with love and respect, and this will make your relationship grow into something filled with love and communication.

When they are young, it is easier to implement this method and you will get better results from it. But that does not mean it cannot be used with older children or teenagers—you can always find a way to ask for things without making claims in all of your relationships—with children, adults, parents, bosses, spouses, and even with yourself.

Now that we know that we can communicate much more effectively with our children when they do something that bothers us. And while this is a process that is not completely realized overnight, it is one that contains satisfactions all along the way. The ultimate result is better relationships between parents and children—relationships based on love and not on power.

Recognizing that we used claims to make others feel bad so that we could feel good will help us become aware of angers that we didn't recognize before; it will help us live in harmony with our loved ones rather than being upset and angry at them. This is one of the most important steps that can lead us to being NEVER MAD AGAIN.

CHAPTER XIII

WORKING WITH THE EGO

Many books discuss the ego: what it is, how it cheats us, and how it keeps us from seeing the world as it is. But many of us see the world, as the ego wants us to see it—distorted by its ideas and concepts.

Understanding the concept of the ego is relatively easy; to learn to stop listening to it is a little more complicated.

For me, enlightenment happens when we stop listening to the ego. It could last forever or just a few moments.

Of course there is no universal solution to getting rid of the ego. The Buddha searched it for many years, then, then he had to starve nearly to death for several days in a cave in order to find enlightenment and get rid of the ego so that he could see the world as it really is—with the eyes of love.

So, trying to find a unique path to enlightenment would only be cheating us.

I have learned that there are many ways people have found throughout history to work with the ego, to learn how to silence it, and to see reality unfiltered, just as it is. All of these ways have something in common, something I call *the ultimate premise*:

IF YOU ARE IN THE PRESENT, THE EGO DOES NOT EXIST.

If you are living consciously in the here and now, the ego disappears. I am not saying it disappears for good; it will return the moment you stop living in the present, making you see the world as it thinks you should. But at those moments when you are present and aware of the moment, the ego cannot show up, because *it only lives in the memories of the past and the promises of the future.* Ego is never in the present—never has been and never will be.

As I mentioned before, there are several ways to get rid of the ego and stay in the present. One of these is an ancient practice used by many religions and spiritual practices around the world; it is the simplest of all, and for me it is the easiest and one of the most effective I know:

Breathing

BREATHING TECHNIQUES

To say that I will now show you some breathing techniques is like telling you to stay in the present. You could say to me:

"Aren't we are always in the present? And aren't we always breathing? So if I'm always breathing and I'm always in the present, then I don't need any techniques to teach me how to do what I'm already doing."

In a way, you are right: your body is always in the present time and your body is always breathing too. Your body can't be anywhere else; it is always in the present.

But your mind is not. It can be anywhere you want it to be, it can be living in the memories of the past or in the promises of the future. That's why you need to learn how to stay in the present and be aware of your breathing at the moment it happens; —the present moment.

So now I tell you:

BREATHE

And of course, you are breathing now, and all the time. Your body is always breathing. If you spend more than a few minutes without breathing, you will die.

What I am asking you to do is to breathe *knowing you are doing it*, feeling your breath, telling your body to breathe, and to stop doing it if you want to stop. This is because when you are doing something consciously—something in the present—body and mind come together in the present moment, and then the miracle arises; you find yourself in a place where there is nothing else but this very moment.

YOU ARE PRESENT

Maybe you've heard somebody talking about raising the consciousness. This used to be seen as a goal only for the enlightened, or for Tibetan monks who work all their lives at raising their consciousness. But I understood that to raise my consciousness, I needed simply to be present, aware of this moment and nothing else.

Enlightenment is having awareness of the moment. It may only be for a few moments, but in those instants, you are present.

YOU ARE AWARE OF YOURSELF AS A WHOLE—MIND AND BODY TOGETHER.

This is the way to recognize that you are present: the moment you find that your mind and your body are in the same moment.

Breathing techniques are meant to show you how it feels when your mind is in the same place as your body.

Let's try this:

Sit for a couple of minutes on a chair, close your eyes, and take three deep breaths, feeling the air passing in through your nose and going out of your mouth. Then open your eyes and feel your body—feel it in this moment. Feel your feet inside your shoes, feel your hips resting on the chair, feel your arms, your hands, your neck, and your head. Then breathe again three times with your eyes open, feeling the air going in and going out.

It is likely that while you were doing this, you had thoughts passing through your mind, try not to get mad because of it, just let them pass and return to breathe. Never mind, that is the ego resisting your intention to stay in the present, even for a minute or two. It doesn't matter—you made it, you stayed in the present, maybe for a couple of seconds, or maybe for a couple of minutes.

Practice this during the day every time you remember it, it only takes a couple of minutes, which your ego will tell you don't have because you can't "waste" two minutes of your busy day! Ignore the ego and do it. If you feel in a hurry, don't worry, just do the first three breathings and go on with your busy day, until you have those couple of minutes.

Exercising breathing six times is the beginning of it; whenever you do the breathing and feel you can do more than three, and then go ahead, there is no limit. The more you feel what it is like to have your mind and body together, the easier it will be to do it more and more often.

I recommend that you do the exercise a few times during the day, but also before you get up and just before you go to bed.

The moment when you are getting up is the moment when your mind is still in the same place as the body, therefore it's the best time to really feel it. And before going to bed, you can relax and prepare your mind to be in your body all night long.

The Buddha taught his disciples:

"Be conscious of every breath you take"

Another powerful way to stop listening to the ego and be present is:

Meditation

INTRODUCTION TO MEDITATION TECHNIQUES:

Meditation is one of the best tools we can have in order to be Never Mad Again, not only because of all the benefits it brings to the mind and body, but because it is a practice of being still. Actually meditation means being still, but not only still, it also means you are not trying to change everything. Not trying to change everything is enlightenment. When we are mad is because we are trying to change the world outside, and if we are not trying to change the world it means we are accepting it as it is, therefore we will not be mad with the world. Meditation teaches us how to be still and not try to change the world, including our own thoughts.

MEDITATION IS PRAYING: Meditation is the way to get in touch with God in silence.

Some people believe that the only way to pray is by talking to God, asking God for help, or repeating prayers, but there isn't just one way to pray. Being in touch with God in silence is one of the strongest ways to pray, it is being in touch with God at the same time we are in touch with ourselves, with our own being. It is talking with God without the need of words, without the need to say anything, yet listening to everything and knowing God from within.

Meditation as prayer leads us to know the peace of God, as Jesus wanted us to see it. To know the love of God is to know God without seeing with our human eyes, without the filters of our human brain, and without the ego's filters.

When we are meditating there is no time, no space, it seems that we are not anywhere, that we are not subject to time but simply exist—that we are one with God.

Meditation is undoubtedly one of the most powerful tools to silence the ego, not only during the time of meditation but over time. If we meditate every day, we are going to silence our ego more and more. Every day, the ego's silence will grow.

There are many techniques for meditation; this is because, as with religion, what works in one culture may not work in another. In my opinion, it doesn't matter which one you use, the important thing is that you meditate.

It is likely that when you begin meditating you will start finding people who already meditate, and maybe someone will try to convince you that the technique they use is the best one for you. Don't worry, it is a natural process—the ego is still trying to survive inside of them. But of course their technique might work for you. Too: try it. If it's not for you, try another, until you find one you like best, and even then be sure eventually to try another.

For me there is no perfect way to meditate; yet all are perfect because they meet the goal of connecting with God.

The easiest way to meditate is to empty your mind. That's it.

Sure, it sounds easy on paper, but our mind has been having thoughts continuously most of the times for most of our life. So what sounds so simple is not, at least at first, because emptying the mind will break the strongest habit our mind has: the habit of thinking.

So it's not so easy, yet it is still simple, and that's the idea you should keep in your mind.

Taking one step at a time, we can create this new habit: emptying our minds, being silent inside, and staying in touch with God without the need to say a word.

First of all: take time to meditate, but never do it as an obligation. The first thing we want to do is to form the new habit, but without getting to the point when we "have" to meditate as an obligation.

"I HAVE to do my meditation at 2:00!"

I understand that to our Western way of seeing things, this kind of regimentation seems normal or necessary in order to start a new task or form a new habit. But with meditation it is different, it is going to be like a new drug. Every time I meditate, I feel peace. In time, you will be convinced that meditation is for you, is something you enjoy doing, and that you can always find time to meditate.

Meditation works best if you do it every day.

You can start with short meditations, maybe for a couple of minutes before getting up or before going to bed, so the habit will be formed, even though is only a couple of minutes. There will be a time when you start to meditate longer—maybe you will find yourself meditating for five or ten minutes, or maybe there will even be times when you do not want to stop meditating.

Ideally, you should not meditate to a predetermined time; instead, let your mind tell you when it is time to bring your meditation to a close.

"Meditation is like diving into the sea; even if you don't get to the bottom of the ocean, you always get wet."

This means that although you may only meditate for a minute, you always get the benefit of meditating for that minute. Maybe you still have thoughts arising throughout the meditation; it doesn't matter, because you always get the benefit. Sometimes you may get the feeling you didn't meditate at all, because you were "thinking" all the time, but because you are meditating, even in those moments when your mind is having thoughts, there is a space between those thoughts, and you get the benefit of that.

You don't understand meditation; you live it. It is impossible to explain in words what is experienced in meditation, and even if I could explain what I experience during meditation, I am not sure someone else has the same experiences I do. Or how do I know we all feel the same when meditating? But one thing I am sure of—being in touch with God is wonderful, it doesn't matter how we experience it, it matters that we are in contact with God.

CHAPTER XIV

MEDITATION TECHNIQUES

Meditation has been practiced for centuries in many cultures, but it is only recently, when Westerners began asking for proof of its benefits, that science started to analyze it. There have been numerous tests performed on people while they are meditating. Many universities around the world now have studies detailing the benefits of meditation.

Broadly speaking, meditation boosts the body's immune system and regulates the cardiovascular system. When we are meditating, our body produces endorphins, which gives us a sense of happiness and well being, but it also retards the aging process of our cells. Meditation improves concentration and reduces stress. Your everyday activities improve the days you meditate.

So if you are really considering meditation, here are some of the most common techniques used today. As I said in the previous chapter, there isn't a single best way to meditate; but try some different techniques until you find the one that is best for you in that moment of your life. If you have a chance to assist to guided meditations in your community, or to meditation classes, I encourage you to do it, as it is easier for some to have a guide in the meditation process.

BREATHING

Although I spoke about breathing as a way to be in the present and stop listening to the ego, breathing is also a well-known method of meditation. It is also the simplest one.

By being aware of your own breathing, you are already in meditation, even for just a few seconds—and sometimes for many minutes.

If you become aware of your breathing and have your eyes closed, and you simply remain aware of the air going in and out, then you are meditating. Your mind's flow of thoughts has stopped, and you have only the awareness of your breath.

At first, as I said before, three conscious breaths are sufficient; you don't have to do it for twenty minutes. We have to understand that we have been used to having one thought after another for years, so when we try to break this habit during meditation, our body may start to feel uncomfortable, and we will return to our habitual current of thought and forget about the breathing.

The most effective breaths involve using the diaphragm. Because most of us are not aware of our breathing throughout the day, we don't realize that most of our breaths are very shallow and fill only a portion of our lungs. These quick shallow breaths release the air quickly.

This kind of breathing affects us in many ways, one of them being our tendency toward a "rushed" life, or immersion in "the rat race." Our breathing reflects the kind of life we have: if we practice calm, deep breathing, then we can't have a rushed life. It is the same with quick, shallow breathing, only in the opposite direction. It is not the breathing that made our life rushed, it is our rushed life that promoted our quick, shallow breathing. In a sense, we don't seem to have time for breathing.

But if you change your breathing to a deep, relaxed pace, you will start to have a calmer life than the one you had with the rushed breathing.

Since we're talking about breathing as a fundamental part of meditation, it is important that we learn again how to breathe.

"The quality of life of any human being will improve by learning again how to breathe just as he did when he was a baby."

All living beings know how to breathe properly from the time they are born, and that includes humans. It is just that humans are the only beings that change their breathing pattern as they grow.

At some moment in our lives—and for most of us, in our youth—we allow ourselves to be influenced by our parents, the environment, the society, television or other influences that make us live life in a hurry; that changes our way of breathing, therefore changing our whole life.

You will see how important breathing is by performing the following exercises:

FIRST EXERCISE:

First take in all the air you can with your nose and mouth, and then hold it for thirty seconds. Try not to let your mind wander, keep it focused only on the seconds passing, keep it only on the clock.

After thirty seconds, let out all the air, and breathe normally. Now repeat the exercise, adding ten seconds, then add ten more seconds each subsequent time, until you reach your limit and you are sure it's the most you can hold your breath.

In the last try, when you can no longer hold your breath, you will realize the importance of breathing. Release the air and breathe normally (if you can); you will have a sense of being alive again, a sense of being saved. SECOND EXERCISE:

Wait a couple of minutes between the first and the second exercise, then:

Sit quietly with your eyes closed and breathe ten times in and out smoothly, breathing at your normal pace. Do not try to take in more air than you normally would and do not stop, just breathe quietly.

Then ask yourself: How do I feel?

Do I feel calm, excited, tired, and happy, at peace, rushed? Only you can answer this question, and you can only answer it by feeling your body.

Upon completion of the ten breaths, stand up and change your natural breathing rhythm to a faster one: take air through the nose and expel it quickly. Do this for twenty continuous breaths without resting.

Once you complete the twenty repetitions, quit breathing fast and breathe, as you need to at the moment—do not try to slow it down, just let your body tell you how much air you need.

Then ask yourself: How do I feel?

Do I feel calm, excited, tired, happy, at peace, rushed? Again, only you can answer this question, and you can only answer it by feeling your body.

Now compare how you felt in both breathing exercises. Try to detect the differences in how your body felt after each exercise.

Now you have experienced how breathing directly affects your body, your mind, and your being.

Viktor Frankl, who survived Auschwitz, wrote a book about what he had learned while he was captive, called *Man's Search for Meaning*. In it he said, "Life isn't something that God gave to us when we were born; God gives us life with every breath."

We are so distracted by our problems that we forget we receive this gift every time we take a breath. We take it for granted. It is the gift of life, and if we do not receive the gift of life for even a couple minutes, we stop living. With the first exercise, you experienced what it is like to not have the gift of breathing, the gift of life.

With these exercises you experienced the importance of breathing for your body. Breathing has the same importance for the spirit, but not just breathing, conscious breathing.

Give yourself the chance to breath consciously ever day, for at least three times during the day, and every time you remember. This simple exercise will prepare you to meditate in the future, and will give you peace of mind and raise your consciousness.

There is also a specific Meditation Technique using breathing, it is the Shambala Meditation, as taught by Chögyam Trungpa. Shambala Meditation is a sit meditation with the eyes open, it seems like a simple technique but it is one of the most powerful meditation techniques. This technique is fully explained in his book "Shambala, The Way of the Warrior", which I recommend reading, not only for the meditation technique, but for the wisdom it could bring.

OBSERVING AN OBJECT

Another technique used in many practices and religions around the world is observing an object.

This method can be used as a preparation for meditation or as a meditation itself. Whether you are already practicing meditation or are new to it, this exercise will start to train your mind to divest itself of thoughts.

Originally the observed object was a candle, which provides a sense of peace to the observer.

The technique is as follows:

Sit comfortably in front of a table, put a lighted candle in front of you, and look at it. Watch the flame of the candle—just watch it, without judgments or thoughts.

Observe it without blinking for as long as you can. After a while your eyes will start to tear, which is the eye's lubrication system, don't worry, just remain calm, the eyes are naturally lubricating themselves.

When you have decided it is time to close your eyes, close them and let your mind remain silent and empty for a moment. You will decide when you are ready to open your eyes and leave the meditation state. At first, you will only be comfortable for a moment with your eyes closed, but after some practice you will begin gradually to increase the time; every subsequent time you will be able to remain quiet, with your eyes closed, because you will feel really comfortable with yourself *doing nothing*, just being silent in God's presence.

At first you should do this for only a couple of minutes, then gradually you can increase the time. I suggest that you try not to be to strictly aware of the time; many of us feel anxiety when we begin "timing" ourselves because doing so leads to thoughts of the future and takes us away from the present moment. Do the exercise for only as long as it is comfortable for you; you may then gradually increase the time, and you will stay relaxed without getting tired or wanting to go on to do other "more important" things.

GUIDED MEDITATION

One of the simplest meditation techniques is the guided meditation. Many stores offer CDs that facilitate guided meditation.

Guided meditations are those in which the narrator leads the practitioner toward a state of peace. Usually peaceful music plays in the background. This kind of practice requires little effort, as the practitioner simply listens to a voice that guides him, step by step, toward a meditative state.

The guided meditations are especially useful for those who have never meditated, or for those who still find it difficult to remain silent inside.

I personally recommend the following authors:

WAYNE DYER

BRIAN L. WEISS

LOUISE L. HAY

ECKHART TOLLE

DEEPAK CHOPRA

Guided meditations are an excellent foundation for other advanced techniques. You will also find authors with advanced meditations, which can help you continue in the meditation process.

NATURE

Another great way to meditate is to be in contact with nature.

Nature is always connected with God, breathes at God's speed, and moves at God's speed. Nature also lives at God's speed and is always in harmony with God.

We are the ones who have given nature a human face, thereby attributing human characteristics to nature. But nature is not like us; nature doesn't have an ego. Everything in nature exists in the present moment.

Nature is always in a meditative state, always talking with God—but without saying anything—and always listening to God in every moment.

In the movie *The Last Samurai,* Ken Watanabe, who has spent his entire life looking for the perfect flower, says to Tom Cruise at the end of the last battle:

"I've been wrong all this time. I was looking for the 'perfect flower' and now I know that all flowers are perfect."

On his deathbed he found enlightenment. He gained the knowledge that not only is everything in nature perfect, that everything in this world is perfect, every moment is perfect, and we are all perfect. Every moment has a purpose in God's consciousness; everything has a purpose, making every moment perfect.

When we are in contact with nature, nature embraces us in its perfect understanding of the present moment, and we are filled with peace and we feel connected to God.

At first, our ego doesn't want to be quiet and begins to judge nature, and to judge your presence there. It puts labels on nature, because the ego believes things cannot exist without a label, therefore it resists your desire to calm down by telling you the labels of the things you see:

"Look at how crooked that tree trunk is, I wonder if anyone made it look like that, maybe when it was only a branch."

"What am I doing here? This is a waste of time; I have many other important things to do."

"There is an olive tree, I wonder if they took the Olive Garden name from one of those trees."

"Right now I should be finishing the work that's waiting for me at the office."

For years we have trained our minds to follow the same current of thought all day long, and we don't know how to stop the flow of thought—to stop thinking.

Because the ego puts labels to everything, we can use this to meditate with nature. In the beginning, when you spend some moments in touch with nature, do the following:

First take three deep breaths with your eyes closed, and then take three more breaths with your eyes open. Then start walking and imagine that you are God and this is the first time you've walked in this garden. Name everything you see. You can use the name you already know or make up new ones for the flowers, grass, and an insect.

Take your time; there is no hurry. Just keep your attention on naming one thing at a time.

Do this for as long as you feel good. When you start to feel anxious or in a hurry, it might be a good time to stop.

With this game, you are telling your ego that *you* are naming things. It then calms down for a while. But as you do one thing at a time, you start to live in the present and nowhere else.

If sometimes you feel that you are too tense, or you want to be in the present again but can't seem to achieve it at the moment, play the game. You don't need to go to a forest (but if you can do it in the nature it will be better); you can walk on the street and do it for five minutes, and it will help you to be in the present.

Then, after a couple of times, you can stop putting labels on things and just be there. You may keep walking, or maybe you'll want to stop and look at a flower or at a tree. You will find yourself immersed in nature's peace and wisdom.

When you accomplish this, then you are in contact not only with nature, but with God too. You will start to feel God's presence in everything, but most importantly, in you.

When you are out in nature, but you can't completely stop the flow of thoughts, there are some things you can do to try to achieve it:

Take three breaths with your eyes closed, keep them closed and just *listen*.

It is possible, of course, that your ego will tell you that your ears are always listening, and in way, that is true: your ears are "listening": but are you aware of what you are hearing? Your mind is so busy listening to its own thoughts that you do not hear what is happening, even when chatting with someone. You believe that you are listening, but even then, the ego is telling you what to answer to what the other person is saying—telling you what will make you right and the other person wrong. In this case, you are not listening to the other person; you're only listening to the ego.

This time you're really going to listen. Close your eyes and listen consciously: detect the sounds around you. A bird singing, the sound of the wind, a river, the waves in the ocean, the sound of rain. At first, you probably will only notice a couple of sounds, but discovering that you can consciously hear these sounds is overwhelming, especially when you realize that they have always been there without your noticing them. Your ears heard them, but your mind didn't, because you were listening to your own thoughts.

Stay there for a while, until your thoughts start to flow again and the sounds disappear—not because they don't exist, but because you stop paying attention to them. When you notice this, then become aware of the sounds again and listen.

Stay there for a while, then slowly open your eyes and *see*.

Seeing is the complement of listening. As before, you know you are always "seeing" (as long as your eyes are open), but you probably are not consciously aware of the things your eyes see. Your eyes are like a camera that is continuously receiving information from the outside world, but your mind is not paying attention because you are watching your own thoughts (in order to have a thought you the brain needs an image) and not seeing what is happening around you.

Lobsang Rampa, in his book, *The Third Eye* tells the story of a Tibetan monk who attained higher levels of consciousness. Among the skills he developed was one that seems impossible: he was able to become invisible.

Rampa explains that the monk did not actually disappear but that because other people were not really seeing him, he was in a sense invisible. He knew that people were too stuck in their own inner dialogues to pay attention to the outside world and to see the people and objects around them. So he would stay very still and become part of the environment. He became "invisible" because he could see how human beings are tied to the ego's thoughts all the time. But another monk, passing by, would see him.

This time, consciously SEE: look closely at a tree or at a plant, a flower, the ocean, the sky, the clouds, a sunset, and a wild animal. Resist the urge to analyze, compare, or judge: just see.

If it is a tree you are looking at, then look closely: see the roughness of its bark, the grooves in its surface, then look at its branches, then its leaves: see how the leaves are a small universe of a different texture and color.

If you are watching an animal, observe how it moves, look at its type of skin or feathers, look at its eyes, notice how it breathes slowly—it seems like it has nothing else to do but just what it is doing right now. It has nothing else planned; it is only living in the present moment. Try to see this, and to feel the animal's presence.

Stay there SEEING until you realize you have returned to your own thoughts and the object you were seeing has disappeared from your conscious mind and your sight and now you can only see a single tree as a whole, without any details, or an animal in the forest, or the ocean.

Congratulations if you managed to do this exercise—you've meditated, you have spoken with God without saying a word, you've experienced God's presence.

It doesn't matter if your thoughts quickly returned to you, and you could only be in touch with nature for a short period of time; a few seconds are enough for you to experience God's presence. This way you can start to meditate and form the habit of quieting your thoughts.

I recommend you do this at every opportunity. If you do it often enough, you will form the habit and your consciously meditating times will grow longer. Do not worry if you think you're not getting there, remember that the more times you remain in contact with nature, the more you will learn from it, the more you will get caught up in its pace. Eventually you will learn that every moment is perfect and that nature is in no hurry at all—just as you could be.

A tree is not worried that its branches are not growing as fast as others' are, it is not concerned that it has not rained this month, the tree simply "is."

If you feel guilty because you haven't had time to meditate, it is the ego that is telling you this; do not listen to it. It is a fact that you will not always have time to meditate. Your mind still has the habit of making you believe you're always busy and do not have time to meditate. In fact you never have time for anything, and meditation may sound like a waste of time—which it literally is. This is one of meditation's benefits: to lose track of time and space, which seems impossible to your mind, which is always counting the time and has an agenda that includes "important" things and can't imagine living any moment unoccupied.

YOGA

Yoga is one of the oldest existing techniques of meditation.

Indeed, although yoga has been understood in the Western world as an exercise of great benefit to health, it actually has a greater spiritual purpose: to promote inner silence.

Yoga is one of six traditional doctrines of Hinduism, which does not mean you have to change religion to practice it.

Yoga is the union of the soul with God, and develops spiritual awareness.

The word yoga comes from Sanskrit and means "yoke," as in the yoke that is used to join two oxen. That is why yoga means to unite our consciousness with God.

There are different schools of yoga, which differ in form but not in their essence and in their purpose.

The most expanded types of yoga in western culture are:

- HATHA YOGA

- KUNDALINI YOGA

Hatha yoga is the most well known worldwide. It is based on positions, which are intended to bring the body to a state of readiness for meditation.

Kundalini yoga is based on simple postures and breathing that requires few physical demands and quickly brings the practitioner to a state of meditation and inner peace

But yoga also provides additional benefits besides inner peace, such as flexibility, strength, and endurance. It also promotes the health of internal organs, relaxes the muscles, and helps strengthen the will and encourage discipline.

Yoga's benefits are great, and you will experience them after only a short period of time.

The best way to practice is in-group classes, which are offered in many cities and towns around the world, but if you do not have access to a class, there are also DVDs and books that teach yoga techniques.

I suggest you practice yoga and experience it for yourself so that you can see if its benefits really are for you.

Yoga is one of the most comprehensive techniques that exist for inner silence and is also one of the most practical. Like the guided meditations, you will be instructed in how to do the poses, and while you are doing them you don't have to make any effort to quiet your thoughts. The postures will guide you to the inner silence you are looking for.

There is a lot of literature available about yoga.

Yoga is one of the more peaceful experiences you can have in this speeding world.

BEING CONSCIOUS OF THE SPACE BETWEEN WORDS AND THOUGHTS

Some other respected authors suggest that you can always meditate if you are only aware of the space between your thoughts. This space is always present between each thought, between each statement, and between each word we speak or think—even in the music we hear: the space between notes is what makes the music harmonious; if there wasn't be any space between notes, you would hear noise instead of melodies.

Try to read the following:

FREQUENTMEDITATIONISAGREATTOOLTOFINDGODIN SIDEOFUSANDRAISEOURLEVELOFCONSCIOUSNESS.

At first our mind sees only a meaningless string of letters. It does not "see" the spaces between the words, and this makes it very difficult for our mind to understand it.

Space is what gives meaning to words.

Also the space between words and thoughts is what gives meaning to our lives—in this space we find God.

FREQUENT MEDITATION IS A GREAT TOOL TO FIND GOD INSIDE OF US AND RAISE OUR LEVEL OF CONSCIOUSNESS.

As Osho said:

"The retirement of the mind is meditation."

When we understand the space between words and thoughts, we become aware, at that moment, that we are pure consciousness, therefore we are in touch with God. There is no alternative; at that moment we are one with God, and there isn't anything else, there isn't the idea of time, space, or matter. None of our ideas of who we are, or what we have, matters: no titles, no names, just pure being.

That is our true nature; this is what we really are. If we remove the skin from a melon, we have the fruit itself. It is the same with us. When we remove all the ideas we have of ourselves—the ideas we have of others, our own ideas of good and bad—then the silence can emerge, the space between ideas, and out of this emerges our true being, the one who we really are, that being that is perfect.

Dr. Wayne Dyer has a method of meditation called "the gap," which he explains in his book Getting in the Gap: Making Conscious Contact with God through Meditation. I urge you to read it, if you believe that gap meditation is for you. Dr. Dyer will guide you all the way through the meditation, so that you visualize the words of a known prayer (the book uses the Lord's Prayer), and while you concentrate and visualize each word separately, you also focus on the space between words and stay there for a while repeating the AH! Mantra. After remaining in that space, you pass to the next word and to the space between that word and the next, and so on. At the end you have meditated for ten or twenty minutes consciously in the presence of God.

In my experience, this is a very simple and practical method of meditation that will introduce you to the experience of silence—perhaps for only a few moments at first but then for longer periods of time. It is a method, which requires no prior experience of meditation.

After some time you will be able to be aware of the space between your thoughts even when you are not meditating.

In order to discover the space between our thoughts, we must be aware that we jump from one thought to another, from an image that is logically connected to another image.

In most of our conversations, it is the same. It is likely that we may start talking about the weather and suddenly shifts to talking about the government without even knowing how we got on to that subject. At some point weather and politics collided; maybe you were talking about a snow storm and then you began talking about the accidents that happened because of the snow, then you started talking about how the government didn't clean up the snow, which led to other things the government doesn't do, and so on.

In your mind, this happens the same all the time. We jump from one thought to another, and then to another, and this goes on all day long, and we don't notice it at all.

In between each thought, there is a space. We don't notice it at the beginning, but it is there. We wouldn't be able to comprehend the image if there wasn't a space. But if we know there is a space, then we start to notice it.

When we discover it, two things happen:

First, these spaces now seem to be longer, so we are becoming increasingly more aware of them, and when we are consciously in those spaces we are connected with God.

The second is that we have fewer thoughts; because the space between thoughts is longer, the time previously needed for a thought is more easily filled.

Whenever we don't have thoughts, we are immersed in silence. Silence is good, even though in our culture silence is usually seen as annoying or even bad. If during a conversation we stop talking, people say that we are having an "awkward moment"; we start to feel nervous and we will try to think quickly of something to say that will break the silence.

When we are quiet for a long time, we begin to feel uncomfortable, even when we are alone.

Religions have taught us wonderful prayers, which we have repeated countless times, and if we really think about what we are repeating, we will find the profound meaning in those words. But we have not been taught to stay in silence and listen to God, our prayers seem to go one way: I talk, and God listen. And he does always listen to our prayers, but rarely do we remain silent in order to hear what God's answer is.

If we learn to embrace the silence, we will find the greatest treasure of all and we will begin to thank God for those moments of silence. We will relearn how to listen, just as when we were babies, and listen to God all the time.

When we are born we are in constant communication with God, we are born connected to God, and we are listening to God all the time. If we look at the face of a sleeping baby, we see its peace. The baby is constantly connected with God. We were all born that way and we all can go back to that place, it is only a matter of embracing the silence and connecting with God again.

Within us all there is a place of peace and love, a place where we meet God and find ourselves, a place without time, space, or form, a place where we feel good and where we need absolutely nothing else, only being. That place is inside of us and at the same time is everywhere; there is God, and when we recognize this place we surrender to a happiness that cannot be explained with words, not the happiness of the body, but pure being in a state of happiness reunited with God. When we get there once, we can go back whenever we want, we can return even after a long time of not being there, because we never really left there, it has always been within us, has always existed in us and we will never part with it; we can forget it, we even can ignore it, but it will never disappear, so at the right time and the exact circumstances, we will rediscover that place within us, then whenever we know it exists and has changed our lives, then our consciousness will rise again, and we rediscover God.

And even though we think we find that place while watching a sunset, or when we are in contact with nature, but in reality, we connect with ourselves in those places. We believe that the sunset gave us peace and that we found God there, but in truth we have found God within ourselves and we learned that when we find him, then we connect with everything else at that moment—we are one with the sunset, which is nothing more than the peace of God. We can only see this when we find ourselves.

In this peace there is no anger, no hatred, in fact there are no feelings, because feelings, as the word implies, are "felt" by the body and in that place of peace, the body does not feel; only love exists—not as a feeling in the body, but as pure love. We don't feel it and our minds can't analyze it—it is just a state of being.

This goes far beyond love as a feeling, it is a love that has no need of being loved in return, it is actually the perfect Love, is all the love of the world and the universe. It does not expect anything, but it is everything.

And all of that is within us, but sometimes we need to find it outside first. It will always be within us and whenever we want we can find it; we always have the possibility of finding it again. Sometimes it will be only a few seconds, but at other times it will seem like an eternity, but not an eternity from the point of view of time, not from the point of view of fear or anxiety, but as an eternity in the never-ending present moment, which is the only thing that exists and that will ever exist. In that moment we are in eternity all the time. We are never really out of it, but our misconception about time tries to take us out and to deny us the true idea of eternity as it really is: the present moment, forever. That is eternity.

CHAPTER XV

FINDING THE SPIRITUAL
SIDE OF ANGER

Anger, in its essence, is the search for oneself.

It is born of the desperation of not finding the self as it really is and not as the ego has told us.

Being angry, viewed from the spiritual side, is being unhappy with who we are. At bottom we are really not angry with anyone but ourselves.

At the moment when we get angry, we are reflecting the fact that we are not happy with ourselves, therefore our anger becomes a kind of inner search, a search for our true being; we get angry because we are not in contact with our being and therefore we feel bad. The ego hides this truth and makes us believe that we are angry with someone else.

The search for our being is not bad, just the opposite; it is great. We only have to realize that anger is a search. Our true self knows that deep inside of us there is something more than what our ego tells us, more than the image the ego projects to us. We know that we are not that image; we know we are much more than that, and that's why we're searching for our real self.

Anger holds wisdom. The spiritual side of anger can help us grow. It is our task to find the truth of what we have always known but that has been kept hidden from us. We have to remember it.

Eckhart Tolle, in his book, The Power of Now, tells the story of how his life changed when he hit bottom. At that moment he realized he could no longer live with "himself"; in that moment he knew that if he could not live with "himself" it meant that there were two people inside him and that one of them must be unreal. He realized that he was the observer and that the other was what he thought he was—that other one was the unreal one, the part that did not really exist. He realized his real being was the one who did not want to live with the unreal image that was created by the ego. At that moment he realized his true self, he realized that everything that had happened before was not bad but rather an intense search of his true being. And in that instant he finally found it.

In essence, we just get angry with ourselves, we can't get angry with anyone else because we are the ones we feel bad. We believe we are the thoughts we have. Well, the other person has his own thoughts, and probably his anger too.

The father who is angry with his son, who broke the camera, is not angry with the child, although it looks like it. He could even take his anger out on the child. But he is angry with himself because he knew that if he left the camera within the child's reach, it was likely that something would happen to it. But he could not accept that reality. Like all of us, he was used to blaming others; he had not learned to take responsibility for his actions. The result is anger.

When we get angry with someone else, we are angry with ourselves, because we couldn't convince others to think like we do. That is the ego telling us we are right and the others wrong.

We don't know or don't want to admit that we are responsible for all of our actions as well as their consequences. We are responsible for everything that happens to us, consciously or unconsciously. But we have been trained since childhood to avoid that responsibility and blame others for what happens to us.

This behavior was mainly learned through imitating our parents and by the way we were taught—scolding and punishment instead of education on the basis of consequences. If we could educate our children with this idea of action, consequences, and responsibility, we would have achieved much, including a much happier family.

Have you ever seen the reaction of some parents in a restaurant when one of the young children accidentally drops a glass of milk or water? First, the parents are angry with themselves for letting the small child take the glass, or maybe they are upset because they had not been watching the child. At the same time, though, they will blame the child, therefore avoiding the responsibility for their actions.

If the child were educated with consequences instead of scolding, the logical step would be to clean up the spilled liquid. The parents could even help the child, or the waiter could help. This way, the child learns that everything has a consequence in life; in this case, the consequence is only a little spill and a clean up. He learns that he is responsible for his actions, that if he spills, then he cleans up. Anger or scolding is not necessary.

He also learns that there are always good people who want to help him in whatever he needs.

As a parent this isn't easy, because we feel observed by others and we feel embarrassed or ashamed that something like this happens in our table, but "something like this" is the consequence of having young children; besides it's great for their learning process, and it is also a consequence of the way we want to educate our children to become responsible for their actions now and in the future.

The other consequence is that we'll have is a happy meal with the whole family, without anger or resentment.

If we take responsibility for our actions from childhood, then we know that our mistakes are not bad, they are opportunities to learn something.

Our mistakes will not be something that will make us feel bad, but they will help us grow as human beings.

When someone fails to yield the right of way and we get mad, it may not be clear at first that we are mad with ourselves because it seems that we are really mad with someone else. But remember the key to recognizing what is happening:

THE ONLY REASON IN THE WORLD YOU GET MAD IS BECAUSE YOU THINK YOU ARE RIGHT, AND THE OTHER PERSON IS WRONG.

Actually you're not angry with those who think differently than you, but you are angered by how you think the other should think. But the other person does not have those thoughts; those thoughts are inside you. You created them, or maybe you've acquired them over the years, but however it happened, they're yours, not the other person's.

You think that if the other person thought differently, you would not be mad. But that is simply wishful thinking: you want them to think your way because you believe that your way is the "right" way.

This is even clearer with our children. Only we can teach them to see the world as we see it, and maybe they will learn by someone else to see the world differently than we do. Eventually they will conflict with us because they do not think like we think, as we have taught them to think.

But we really have no other way to teach than by the way we see the world. Much of our learning is formed by the society in which we live. For example, if your child burps at the table you will probably tell him to not do it again because it's bad manners in our culture, but if we were living in a Middle Eastern country and we did not burp when we were eating, our fathers would be displeased because burping is a way to thank the host and say that we liked the food we were eating. Similarly when we have a baby who does not burp after drinking a bottle, we strive to make him burp, and if he can't, we even will take him to the doctor to tell us why he can't burp.

It's a habit we have acquired from our culture, and learned primarily from our parents.

So we teach our children what we believe is best for them, so that they can be happy. Many of the things we teach are sure to give happiness, but some are just wishes; we think about the things we didn't do that could have made us happier.

So, when we get angry with our children, we are not angry with them but with our idea of how they should be, therefore we are mad with ourselves for not having taught them to act in the way that we believe is right. But we hold on to the idea of how they "should" act or how they "should" be educated.

It's always about us, about our ideas, and our way of seeing good and bad, right and wrong.

If we had a specific idea of something, then if someone does not agree with that idea, we get angry, as in the case of the Middle Eastern child who burps as a polite way of saying thank you. If we had not acquired the idea that burping is bad, we would not need to be angry. In fact, as we know with the infants, burping is good for our health, but our society at some point decided it was rude and now we have to obey the rules, even if they are against our own digestion.

We can live in peace with ourselves and not have to be angry. If we live with peace of mind, in constant contact with our being, then there will be no need to get angry. Our search for ourselves is not through anger; it will be through living day to day in contact with our true being.

As I mentioned before here is a premise that can help us have a spiritual point of view of life, a premise that can help us to see the world in a way we would not have the need to be angry again:

Everything happens for our own sake.

This concept may be one of the most difficult to understand, but it may be the most powerful if we truly believe it from the bottom of our heart. If we do, then not only will we stop having the need to get angry, but we will have a fulfilled life in everything that we do, as we will be living it with all of our senses open to the opportunities that are presented to us in every moment.

"When God closes a window, he opens a door"

But so often we only see the closed window, and we even blame God for closing the window. We keep our attention on the closed window, unable to turn to the opposite side of the room and see the great door that God has opened for us. If that window hadn't been closed, the door could have not been opened to us.

Whoever understands this will have a life in which concerns are transformed into opportunities, where problems are only road signs that tell us that something better is coming, that something bigger than our understanding is organizing it, and that if we pay attention to the possibilities we will see the path that is opening in front of us.

I once read that trust is nothing more than putting our attention only in what we want to happen to us.

For me faith is nothing more than to know that the best is always going to happen to us, even if we don't understand it at that time.

Jesus said that faith moves mountains, not only the faith of knowing that God exists, but the knowledge that God has always prepared the best for us, that we ourselves are the ones who attract what we want by putting our attention on it. If we stop spending most of our time thinking about what bothers us and about what we don't want for our lives, we will begin attracting to ourselves what we really want in our lives.

CHAPTER XVI

THE MOST IMPORTANT TIME IS "NOW"

Realize deeply that the present moment is all you have. Make the NOW the primary focus of your life.

Eckhart Tolle

The easiest way to live a life without anger is by realizing this:

The most important moment is now.

It sounds extremely easy to follow—and it is easy, but it is not simple.

It is not easy because our ego is trying to distract us at every moment, the ego wants to live in the past or in the future, but never in the present, because in the present, the ego does not exist; in the present, the ego dies.

The ultimate goal of the ego is to survive, and the ego cannot survive in the present. If we were ever present, the ego would diminish in our minds, because we would not have time to listen to it, we would be in the now and could never hear it.

Living in the present and not listening to the ego does not mean that the ego just disappears, it means we are so immersed in the present moment that we don't have time to listen to it; it would be like those times when you have a pain in the body, a pain that bothers you, but if you start doing something really important, something that demands your full attention, then you forget about the pain. It does not mean that the pain no longer exists, the pain is still there, it's simply that you don't have time to focus on the pain, so it loses its strength and no longer has the importance it had when you were paying attention only to it.

It you live in the present, it is practically impossible to be angry.

When the other driver crossed in front of us, we felt anger because the other person did something wrong according to our way of thinking. At that moment the ego is in top form and giving us all the possible arguments to make the other person "wrong" and us "right." The ego is trying to keep us living in the past. But the instant following the incident was a new moment; if we didn't listen to the ego, we would just keep driving as we were minutes before, unbothered. We would arrive home and have dinner, just as on any other day.

Anger and resentment live in the past, but not in the present. Resentment can't live in the present because it feeds only on the past and carries that resentment forward in the form of revenge toward the people who hurt us.

The easiest way to live without anger is to live in the present moment. It is not easy at first, but if you get used to it you will live in the present and stop getting angry. Then, as Jesus said, "the kingdom of God is yours," here on earth, in every moment.

The present is a gift and that's why it is called a "present." It is the gift of life that God gives us every moment, with every breath and every heartbeat.

Living in the present is the easiest way to enlightenment, since at the moment we are present it is as if we illuminate the room, we are able to see everything clearly, and we no longer need to listen to the ego. We can see things as they are and not through the filters of the ego.

Early in the book I mentioned that if you find this book somewhere, start reading, and do not buy it, I would be happy if you could understand only the phrase

THE ONLY REASON IN THE WORLD YOU GET MAD IS BECAUSE YOU THINK YOU ARE RIGHT, AND THE OTHER PERSON IS WRONG.

Well, I tell you now that you've almost finished the book:

If you could remember and implement only one of the techniques in this book, it would be this:

THE ONLY IMPORTANT THING IN YOUR LIFE IS "THE PRESENT MOMENT"

It is not only the most important thing, it is really the only one, because it involves everything else in your life that you believe is important, and the most important one is that God is here in the now all the time. The only place where you can find God is in the now.

This is one of the wisest things ever to be said. It is not mine but has existed in all religions and has been underestimated through the years.

Remember when Jesus said:

"Do not think about tomorrow, each day has enough with its ideal."

Jesus was teaching us to live in the now. Jesus lived his life in the present.

Jesus also had a human side, also got mad, as the Bible tells us; but there are two things to consider when we analyze Jesus' anger:

The first is that if Jesus got angry with the merchants in the Temple, I believe it was because he wanted to give us a specific lesson.

Jesus wanted to take the merchants out of the Temple—but he was not referring to the Temple as a church, but as the temple of God, which is each of us, the spiritual temple.

The merchants represent the market that exists inside of our temple: the ego with all its false beliefs that lead us away from the real temple that we are and into the endless current of thoughts, one after another without a break. These are the merchants inside our temple that make the noise that distracts us from the present and takes us away from God.

The second, even more important than the first, is that although Jesus was angry, he never had resentment, because Jesus always lived in the now. When the Bible tells us that he drove the merchants out of the Temple, it says he told them to leave his Father's temple. The Bible does not say that Jesus shouted at them every time he saw them or that he was very angry for a week because of the incident of the Temple. He only got angry at that moment, the moment passed, and Jesus entered into the Temple to pray. When he was praying, he wasn't angry anymore; Jesus was living only in the present moment, and getting angry was just another way to show us the way.

Once you get the merchants out of your temple, you enter into a deep prayer with God all the time; there is no longer the noise that distracts us from God. It doesn't mean that if there is noise God is not there; God is always there; it is only that the noise occupies our attention so that we do not realize that God is always with us.

Fear is another part of the ego that cannot live in the present, because it feeds on assumptions about things that may occur in the future, based on past events and enhanced by the power of imagination.

Resentment is based on fear; resentment is the aspect of the ego that is afraid of not being "right."

Recently a friend of my wife ran into a woman with whom she had been in kindergarten. My wife's friend told her that she could not stand that woman because she had pulled her hair when they were five years old, and she couldn't forget it. That is resentment.

The resentment she had toward the other woman had been stored for many years, and when she saw her, she not only remembered the past but felt the resentment she had felt back then. Her ego felt once again the same fear for itself that it had felt thirty years earlier, so the ego sent the same feeling again so that she could feel the need to be "right" and the other person "wrong" for what she did all those years ago.

The resentment lies in remembering what someone did to us in the past and to try to harm that person in the future. But if we live in the present, we cannot be bitter about the past or think about how we can make that person feel bad in the future, because those things are not in the now.

THE PRESENT IS FORGIVENESS

The present is forgiveness with no struggle; it is a peace that frees us from the ego and any resentment, without any effort.

Leo Tolstoy wrote:

"Most of my life I have lived in fear of the problems in my life, but most of them never happened."

Fear is the master of the future and the past, fear takes us to the future in a negative way, collecting past events or collecting experiences to justify its existence.

Fear is the ego's tool. The ego is basically fear itself, because the ego is afraid all the time.

Fear is lack of presence; therefore ego is lack of presence too.

FORGIVENESS IS RECOGNIZING THE INSUBSTANTIALITY OF THE PAST

Forgiveness recognizes that the past has no substance; it recognizes that the past does not exist; it existed as present at some point, but in this moment it is only an image.

Imagine for a moment that you are in a movie theater watching a 3-D movie, and because the images on the screen feel so real, you try to touch them. But you cannot touch the pictures; you cannot touch the actors, because what you're seeing is just the images, not the actors themselves. Even though they seem real, images have no substance; they are like a projection of light.

The same is true of the past. We can't touch the past because it does not exist as something substantial; it exists only as an image in our minds. All we can touch is what we have before us at this time and nothing more—there is nothing outside the present that you can touch; you can only touch the present moment.

Remember the example of the lime? The past is the same. Our brain sees an image and sends the image stimuli that is being generated, but that does not mean that these are real; there never was a lime in your hands or in your mouth, but it felt to your body as though it were real.

Past and future have the same effect; that is why you feel bad if you remember something unpleasant from the past. You can also feel bad if you imagine something unpleasant that could happen in the future, but neither of them exists.

They are only images and therefore they are not real. The only reality that exists is here and now. This is the essence of forgiveness: if we understand that the past is just an image that we have in our brain, then we will realize that past events that bothered us or made us mad do not exist now. And because we can only forgive what is real, we don't have anything to forgive.

If we understand this, then forgiveness will not be something that we "have" to do but will be something to live with naturally in every moment. This will give us peace without any effort or any sacrifice, all because we are present at this moment.

The ego is not only responsible for projecting the images of past and future but is also the director of the film. We really have no control over what we're thinking most of the time, we only see the images moving one after another, and the ego is directing the film in every moment.

The ego directs the film you see in your life; therefore, the ego directs your life. The only way to stop this film is to be present; in the present the ego cannot run anything or project anything, because the ego does not exist in the present. It is just another image we cannot touch, because it is not real; the essence of ego is the images we have of ourselves and the images others have of us.

The ego is itself just another movie—a movie from the past.

The ego's projections are like those times when you go to a movie theater. You watch the movie intensely, and meanwhile it has been raining outside, so at the end of the movie you go out and realize it has been raining—but of course you didn't notice it. Imagine that the present is what is happening outside of the movie theater and the theater is your mind where you are watching the images the ego is projecting. You really can't be in both places; you can't watch the movie and the rain at the same time. In the same way, you cannot be watching the ego's images and also be in the present, and you cannot be in the present and also watch the movie presented by the ego. Neither of them exists in the world of the other.

This is how the ego works.

Most of the time, you believe you are in the present, but you are not. You believe all you are doing is watching the movie, but you can watch the movie and at the same time keep your mind somewhere else, thinking about the rain and all the things that can happen when it rains: my clothes are going to get wet, the garden is going to be muddy, the car will get dirty and I just washed it. That is how the ego makes you believe you are present, and yet your mind is elsewhere, whether in the past or the future, but never in the present.

As you noticed, several times I have repeated the concept that the ego lives in the past or in the future but never in the present. This will help us to find out what the ego is doing at this moment. Right now you can stop reading the book and sit there doing nothing. In a couple of seconds you will start to think of something, your ego will try to get you out of the present at any price. You will start to remember things that need doing.

If you are in the present, the ego dies, therefore it does its best to survive, that is the reason most people can't be still and do nothing but sitting.

When you enter a doctor's waiting room you can see that everybody is "doing" something—reading a magazine, doing something with the phone, talking on the phone—because people can't tolerate the idea of doing nothing (that's the reason they have magazines). We think doing nothing is a waste of time, and we believe that society has made us think that way because of the ideas we have about productivity. But this is not true; the ego is the one that can't live without doing something. The ego needs to be busy doing something and thinking about something, but the ego does not want you to do something that requires you to focus or concentrate; it wants you to do something that will disconnect you from the present and the present's gift of possibility: that you will begin to think about who you really are. At times when you have nothing to do, the ego sends you a sense of guilt so that you'll feel guilty for doing nothing.

Do you know the saying that says, "Leisure is the mother of all vices"? On the contrary, if we take leisure as an opportunity at certain times to do nothing (of course, not all day), just to remain quietly in our room without paying attention to the ego, and to watch all the thoughts that might pass through our mind, then we will begin to feel better. We will be connected with God more often than with the ego.

LET THE EGO GO

The ego is an addiction that all mankind suffers from, but like all addictions, if we can liberate ourselves from it, it will strengthen us and lead us to a new life far better than the one we had. Many people who are freed from an addiction thank God that they had the addiction, because they find true life only after being set free.

Getting free of the ego is a bigger job than kicking any other addiction, and as with others addictions, the first step is admitting that you are addicted.

When we become aware that we are addicted to the ego, we have taken the first step, but not even the first step ensures that we will free ourselves of the ego. Very few people are aware that they are the ego's slaves.

When my oldest son was six years old, he asked me if the ego was the devil. I replied by asking him what he thought about it, and he said he did not know. I forgot about it, but the next day while I was driving the kids to school, he suddenly said

"Dad, now I know that the ego is really the devil."

End of the story. He didn't say anything else, but he sounded so convinced that I pondered it for a while.

I am convinced that young children have a much stronger connection with God and with wisdom than adults do, mainly because their minds are not yet filled with all the beliefs and rules that adults have accumulated. If we listen carefully to children, they will surprise us with their wisdom. But we are often so blinded by our idea of our responsibility as parents that we believe we are the only ones that can teach them.

Now, is the ego really the devil?

First let's dispense with the image that we had from childhood of the devil as a person with horns and tail, red skin and a goatee beard, holding a pitchfork, who lives in the flames and comes to earth for the sole purpose of convincing us to do bad things.

I don't know the origin of this picture, but it was probably used to instill fear in and impose control over "bad" people.

Likewise, God is not an old man sitting on a throne holding a staff in his hand, which is the image that many Christians come to have of God. But God cannot be expressed with images, because images cannot cover everything that God is, neither we can put that in a sculpture or a painting. But God, being omnipresent, is in that painting too.

Once we know that the image we had of the devil is just an image that someone invented at a certain time in history, now we can find something like the concept of what might be the devil.

We have the belief that the devil gets inside our heads and tells us to do something bad. He tells us not to listen to God; therefore he tries to make us disconnect ourselves from God.

I also like the image of the devil as he appears in cartoons, where there is a character who has the devil in his left ear and an angel in the other ear. The devil is constantly telling to do what is wrong (and to not listen to what the angel on the other side is saying to us), and even though the character always knows that the angel is right, he does not always listens to him; he listens to the devil and he gets in trouble for doing so.

If this is a good definition of the devil, then the ego fits neatly into it, and although the ego does not seem as bad as the devil, the ego is the one who tells us to turn away from God. The ego is the one who defines for us who we are or what he have achieved (pride), that we are what we have (greed), that if we lose what we are or what we have we will be very bad (selfish), and that if someone thinks differently from us, that person is wrong and we are right (anger).

The ego is constantly telling us things but it never tells us to connect to God. The ego knows that if we connect to God, it cannot exist.

On the other side is the "angel," who represents who we really are, is always in connection with God.

So for me, the ego has the same personality and characteristics of the one we have been taught to call the devil, or the evil. But the ego is not to be feared; rather, our awareness will help us eradicate the ego from our minds.

Many people have regrets about something they did or something they are ashamed of, something "bad" that they may have done only once. But this feeling is of the ego, not the devil. It can even be something small, such as eating an ice cream cone when they knew they shouldn't have.

SEPARATION IS THE FOUNDATION OF THE EGO'S IDENTITY

The ego bases its fears in the sense of separation. To the ego, we are all independent beings separate from one another, and in this world-view, the ego is right at home, because all of our egos are separate and independent of others'; each one has his own ideas of who he or she is.

That is the main reason we have problems with others and why we get mad: each ego is independent and "different" (but not really) and each believes he is right and the others are wrong.

This is how the ego would have us believe the world is made: billions of people, all separate from one another, all independent of each other, and, even though we all live in the same world, all separated from the world!

And that's just how we see it most of the time because we listen to the ego most of the time. We see each person separated from every other person. We know that some people are like us in their way of thinking, we know there are people who have things in common with us, but nevertheless we see all of them separately, and we see ourselves separate from others.

This is how the ego has taught us to see the world, because it is perfect for the ego. For the ego this is not a lie, this is just how it really sees the world, for the ego exists only for what it is, for what it has accomplished, for what it owns, and for what others think of it.

Here is the truth that the ego cannot see:

WE ARE ALL CONNECTED, AND EVERYONE IS CONNECTED TO GOD, THEREFORE WE ARE ONE.

We are one, but with different paths and roles in this world and we exist in different forms, but we have the same essence, so we are essentially all the same.

Let's look at an analogy of what we are.

With a sheet of paper or a book cover the palm of your hand so that you can only see the fingers—not the palm, only the fingers. Put it in front of you. You see your fingers as independent of the others, but if you take down the sheet you will see the fingers as they really are, bound together by the palm of the hand. You see the hand as one, with several parts, but in the end, a whole.

We are all like the palm, we are all united by God, but we seem to be independent from each other; the ego has made us see others and ourselves as though we are each independent and separate, but if we remove the veil of ego we see how we really are: all linked together in God.

Now, although the ego seems to be God's enemy, this is true for the ego but not for God. If we stay consciously connected with God in the present moment, the ego dies. All of the ego's actions are designed with the ultimate goal of survival in mind. All the thoughts we have—of selfishness, greed, envy, and fear—are ego-thoughts, devised by the ego to avoid its own death.

And although the ego seems to be the devil and appears to be strong, it is not; the ego is just a frightened child who is afraid, whose whole life has been lived in fear, who knows no other feeling besides fear.

So is the ego a bad thing?

For a long time I had trouble understanding why God created the ego, why God in his infinite wisdom had sent everyone to earth with an ego. Why would God have invented the ego—the only thing that takes us away from our true nature and from God, brings us into conflict with each other, and creates wars between nations, between individuals, causing humanity to suffer constantly?

The ego is the cause of our suffering, not pain; pain is something you feel physically. But suffering is formed in the mind and then transmitted to the body by the ego.

Why would God want us to suffer?

For me it wasn't a complaint, it was a doubt, something I could not understand, something beyond me. I started to think about it often, but I could not find an answer.

Until one day, it came to me:

"The ego helps us learn what we came to this world to do and it does so by interacting with the egos of the others."

Then I realized that the ego was a teacher and not an enemy, that God did not create it—we created it ourselves before we came to earth. Before we came here, we chose the ego that we wanted to have so that we could learn what we needed to learn. The ego is a teacher and when its students learn the necessary lesson, the ego disappears.

I realized that we learn from others' egos; only by interacting with them can we learn our lesson. I recognized that dealing with others' egos makes learning more difficult, that this difficulty is necessary. It would be impossible for our ego to be formed if it were not for the egos of others.

I understood that the ego is not bad; I stopped seeing the ego as powerful and evil and started to look at it as if it were a child, a child who lives full of fear, a child who is always about to cry—a child who does not know how to free himself from his fear and so does everything he can to stop that feeling.

There is a story that illustrates why the ego exists:

In ancient Vedic books, the legend is that human life is just a game that God made for himself, and that the meaning of the game is for God to recognize himself again. Then he created the ego to distract us from our true nature, so that we forget that we are God, and thus began the game of life, which has the ultimate end of recognizing that we are God.

If we live in the present, if we live each moment in God, then we will have freedom from the ego. We will release this child from his fears and from then on that small child will live only on love, and because in love there is no fear, he will be fearless in God.

And if God is love and in love there is no fear, and if it is fear that makes us mad through the ego, then we will never get mad again.

That is the end of the ego: when we become aware of God within us and recognize ourselves again in this game of life, we recognize we are God.

Now that we recognize ourselves as we are, we see ourselves as part of God—as loving beings free from fear, free from the ego. We are now ready to accomplish the purpose for which ego was created in the first place—to help us become conscious of God.

From now on, we'll be mad no more. We will see ourselves as the whole hand, not just the fingers, we will recognize that God is in everyone and that everyone has an ego that believes it is right all the time. Knowing this will set us free from our own ego, free from our anger and our fears, and we will live in God in this moment—and all the time.

So be it.